DISCOVERING YOU

TIM ANDERSON

Discovering You
Tim Anderson

Copyright © 2020 Tim Anderson.

All rights reserved solely by the copyright holder. The copyright holder guarantees all contents are original and do not infringe upon the legal rights of any other person or work. No part of this book may be reproduced or transmitted in any form or by any means, electronic or mechanical, including photocopying, recording or by any information storage and retrieval system, without the permission of the copyright holder or the publisher.

Published by OS Press - Fuquay-Varina, NC

ISBN: 978-1-64184-351-5 (Hardcover)
ISBN: 978-1-64184-352-2 (Paperback)
ISBN: 978-1-64184-353-9 (ebook)

Thank you to JETLAUNCH.net for editing and book design.

CONTENTS

An Open Invitation 1

As You Were, So You Are 7

I Am 13
    Using What You Have 16

The Truth Behind Legends 20
    The Fountain of Youth 22

The Miraculous Machine 24
    The Origin of Longevity 27
    The Three Pillars of Human Movement 29
        Pillar #1: The Breath of Life 29
        Pillar #2: The Balance of It All 33
        Pillar #3: The Secret of the X 37

The Other Major Sources of Information 41
Holding Your Tongue 42
The Mind and Our Thoughts 45
The DNA of the Soul 46
Programming Our DNA 50

The Spirit of You(th) 55
The 15 Commitments of Conscious Power 58
I Walk the Line 58
The Power of Truth 61
"This is the Way" - The Mandalorian Creed 62

Are We What We Eat? 69
The Miracle of Eating 71

The Kingdom of You(th) 77

A Daily Movement Routine 80
The Daily 21s for Vitality 82
The Daily 21s for Strength and Wellbeing 102
21s for Life 128

A Daily Being Routine 129
Practice Being 130
Forever You(ng) 133

DISCLAIMER!

You must get your physician's approval before beginning this exercise program.

These recommendations are not medical guidelines but are for educational purposes only. You must consult your physician prior to starting this program or if you have any medical condition or injury that is contraindicated to performing physical activity. This program is designed for healthy individuals eighteen years and older only.

See your physician before starting any exercise or nutrition program. If you are taking any medications, you must talk to your physician before starting any exercise program, including *Discovering You*. If you experience any lightheadedness, dizziness, or shortness of breath while exercising, stop the movement and consult a physician.

It is strongly recommended that you have a complete physical examination if you live a sedentary lifestyle, have high cholesterol, high blood pressure, diabetes, are overweight, or if you are over thirty years old. Please discuss all nutritional changes with your physician or a registered dietician. If your physician recommends that you not use *Discovering You*, please follow your doctor's orders.

All forms of exercise pose some inherent risks. The authors, editors, and publishers advise readers to take full responsibility for their safety and know their limits. When using the exercises in this program, do not take risks beyond your level of experience, aptitude, training, and fitness. The exercises and dietary programs in this book are not intended as a substitute for any exercise routine, treatment, or dietary regimen prescribed by your physician.

THANK YOU

Joshua Edwards, thank you for teaching me how to ask questions and taking me out of my comfort zone.

Trey Baker, this has been the best cup of coffee I have ever had. Thank you.

AN OPEN INVITATION

By nature, we are information gatherers, physically and mentally. Physically, our nervous system craves information, and with the information it receives, it builds itself and expresses itself through the body—the very body that it also generates from this constant incoming information.

Mentally, our minds crave information in the form of knowledge and understanding. From the information our minds accumulate, we construct a mental framework of how the world operates. This mental framework gives us boundaries and keeps us "safe" from the unknowns in the world. Most of us don't like unknowns, so we search, or collect, or cling to information that helps us make sense of the world. Most of the time, this information is taught to us; some of the time, we learn this information through experience or our interpretation of experience.

As far as knowledge goes, we are born into this world as both a blank canvas and a quenchless sponge. We are boundless beings of energy, and we are wide open and ready to receive all incoming information. As a result, we begin to take the shape of what we learn, or we construct a framework to process what we learn *based on what we learn.*

Think about this. When you were born, you were full of limitless energy and life. But you weren't full of knowledge. You had an immense thirst for curiosity, and everything you came into contact with, every brand new experience, became information. Most of this information delighted your soul and fueled even more curiosity. You could think and learn, yet you didn't think with words because you couldn't until you learned them.

Have you ever pondered this? There was a time when you knew how to think without the framework of words.

But then, you did learn words. And along with words, you learned their meanings and definitions. And then, you learned to think by using those meanings and definitions. Another way to say this is that you learned to think by using those labels, those lids, and those limitations. Words are necessary, don't get me wrong; I LOVE words! But words can be limiting or damaging, depending on the meanings, definitions, and images they begin to carry.

And, depending on our environment, the words we learned as children more than likely all came from perceived views, opinions, beliefs, backgrounds, and cultures. This is crucial to ponder because all of us have grown from limitless thought without the use of a language framework to a constructed way of thinking built on the framework of words we have learned from the interpretations, perceptions, intentions, beliefs, and opinions of others. Yes, to people of a common language, "ball" means a round sphere that could potentially be played with, but even the labels and definitions of words can take on a different meaning depending on how they are delivered and with what intent they are taught.

All I'm trying to say is that we learn words and lessons that are fed to us as children, and we have no way to filter out the truth from the lies because we are sponges craving to be filled. Naturally, we are born believers. It's all true until something happens to shake our "belief tree." But this doesn't happen for many, many people. Many people go through life only thinking within the framework of what they were taught as children. They learn how to receive information, but they don't learn how to weigh it and decipher it. As a result, they cling to their tree of belief and attack anything that seems to fall outside of their framework of belief or understanding.

This is the reason for most disagreements between people, countries, and religions. We get stuck in our comfortable framework, the framework we have learned, the framework that we have allowed to define who we are. As a result, many of us become rigid in thought and inflexible. We become incapable of listening to diverse opinions, incapable of empathizing with others who are different from us, and we become closed-minded or hard-hearted. Yet, when we were born, we were completely open-minded and soft-hearted, ready to receive information with joy and wonder.

This was me. I have been guilty of holding onto things that I was told. I have been guilty of not knowing how to weigh information and discern the greatest good for all people. As a result, I have been selfish, close-minded, insensitive, and thoughtless toward others. I've been blind to the freedom of truth and the joys of making discoveries.

But thankfully, I have had my belief tree shaken many times in the past few years. Here is just one silly yet paradigm-shifting example:

I grew up in the Bible Belt of the southeast region of the United States. That means I was a Southern Baptist. As a young Southern Baptist, I was taught things that I could not question. Or at least I was taught that I should not question certain things. Anyway, I was taught that humans were God's greatest creation. We were the pinnacle, his pride and joy. God made everything, but we were special, and he gave us souls. I was also taught that animals didn't have souls.

All my life, I operated in that framework of knowledge that I had collected. And it's funny; deep inside, something within me didn't resonate with that, and I often felt it. The movie *All Dogs Go to Heaven* pushed against my mental framework. How can dogs go to heaven if they don't have souls? *Or,* what if the movie is right? What if all dogs do go to heaven? If that's the case, why don't all people go to heaven? With such a rigid mental framework, silly things like movie titles fell outside of my understanding, so I either dismissed them or attacked them. But what did I know except what I was taught? And no, in case you're wondering, I never thought anything bad about people who liked *All Dogs Go to Heaven*. I'm just illustrating how rigid I once was.

But then, some years ago, something happened that shook my belief tree hard enough to break some branches: I witnessed a cow funeral.

My property backs up to a cow pasture. One day, my wife and I noticed there was a sick cow in the pasture. It didn't look healthy, and it moaned in pain and agony. The other cows in the pasture also seemed to be trying to push it away and kick it out. It was an interesting sight to see. It was as if they didn't want to be around it.

A couple of days later, the cow died, and my wife and I witnessed one of the most amazing things I've ever seen. The entire lot of cows gathered together in a huddle, and all of them faced the dead cow, which was lying on the ground about fifteen yards away. Then, one cow walked over to the dead cow, lowered his head to the cow, paused for a moment, and then turned around and walked back to the herd. Another cow did the same thing. One by one, each cow walked out to the dead cow and lowered their head to it as if to say goodbye. That was one moment of many where I learned that there was much more to this life than I had been taught to believe.

I know that seems like a fanciful story, and it is, but it is also a real event that I witnessed. It is an event that helped break my mind free from some of its rigid constructs. The cow funeral helped to open my mind to a greater possibility. Perhaps all dogs do go to heaven. Perhaps all cows do go to heaven. Wait…perhaps all people do, too.

Why am I telling you this? Because I want to invite you to lay aside all that you think you know and be open to greater possibilities. "Lay aside" may be too heavy. Perhaps "loosely hold on to" what you know may be easier to handle. Frequently, what we know keeps us from learning new things. To put this more bluntly, usually, the lies we rest on keep us from discovering the truth. You were born with a very open mind. What if you were never supposed to lose it? What if your quenchless curiosity was never meant to be replaced with limited and rigid definitions, thought patterns, and ideas?

If we are clinging to ideals, we can't learn anything new. If we are holding onto lies, believing them to be true, we will never find the freedom of truth.

In this book, I'm going to attempt to expose you to some wild possibilities and thoughts about how your body is supposed to age, or not age. I am asking that you be open enough to weigh them and discern if they are true or not. I am appealing to the child inside of you, the one curious to learn from wonder and the one bold enough to seek adventure.

I'm going to quote the Bible, Buddha, and random people you don't know. I may even quote a movie or two. I do that because I am familiar with them as they are, and were, a part of my mental framework—my now flexible and pliable mental framework.

We were born open-minded, a pristine blank canvas. What if we were meant to be an unblemished blank canvas every day of our lives?

Along with that, we were born with boundless energy and vitality. What if we were meant to live with that same vibrancy every day of our lives as well? Perhaps we were.

You're not meant to grow old, weary, and weak. What if that were true? What if you could live your entire life with the same vitality and youth you had as a child? Would you be open enough to entertain that idea?

If cows can have funerals, anything is possible.

AS YOU WERE, SO YOU ARE

If you've read any of my other books, you know that I'm a Superman fanboy. At forty-four, I want to be Superman when I grow up. In fact, I've written a whole book *(The Becoming Bulletproof Project)* about how to realize our full potential and release the superhero inside of us. We were all destined for great things, and we all have immeasurable potential. I believe this is why so many of us love superheroes; we are heroes, even if we don't realize it.

However, as superheroes go, not everyone shares my love for Superman. People who criticize Superman usually don't like him because they may think he is overpowered, or they think he doesn't have any weaknesses. But that's not true. Superman's power is proportional to the need of the moment. Yes, he gets his power from the Sun, and yes, it can give him limitless ability, but he never really discovers the power he has until the movement is needed. This is perhaps one of the most beautiful parallels between Superman and our real lives, as we often don't know what we are capable of until the moment arises that begs our capability.

And Superman is not without weaknesses. He has two major weaknesses: compassion and kryptonite. Compassion is a tremendous weakness. It can lead you to put others before yourself, to harm yourself for the sake of others. Compassion can even get you killed. I read somewhere that there is no greater love than compassion. Perhaps that also means there is no greater pain than compassion.

In a sense, compassion is like Superman's emotional kryptonite. I imagine it's emotional kryptonite for all of us; it drives us to the rescue, to know what we are made of, to give ourselves for another, to perhaps even harm ourselves or die for another. Wait, having just written this, I now realize compassion isn't a weakness at all. It's a strength. It reveals our vulnerability, which leads to invulnerability. I know that's confusing, but willing or allowing ourselves to be vulnerable (compassion is a willingness) makes us all invulnerable. So scratch that. Compassion cannot be a weakness of Superman, nor can it be a weakness of ours.

So I guess that brings us to green kryptonite, Superman's one true weakness. Green kryptonite is the check that balances Superman's power because it can kill him. You might be thinking, *Yeah, but Superman rarely comes into contact with green kryptonite, and he always gets away from it and recovers.* Yes, but it only takes one encounter with something that can kill you, with something that robs your power or almost takes your life away, to really harm you. Once the knowledge of physical vulnerability is discovered, it can create a greater, lasting emotional damage than the object that caused the physical damage in the first place. The emotional and mental pain caused by physical pain can be quite difficult to overcome.

Think about it. If you knew you were invulnerable, but you somehow got introduced to pain, sickness, or the brink of death, what would that do for your psyche? Would it bury you in fear? Or would you dust off your cape and learn to fly again, higher than ever before? Some of you reading this know what I'm talking about. Some of you have been really sick at some point in your life, seriously sick. Some of you have been seriously injured before, and maybe near death. Severe sickness, severe pain, severe accidents, severe loss—they can bring a different type of clarity that is hard to describe. Getting to the other side of an incidence of ill health can be quite a blessing as it offers a sober account of the value and joy of good health. One of my mantras is, "It feels good to feel good." And while that seems like a no-brainer, it always grows in deeper clarity each time I find myself in a "bad way."

I suspect you know this, but it does indeed feel good to feel good. There may be no greater gift than feeling good and having good health. Well, except for the gift of *knowing* the value of feeling good and having good health. Once we encounter kryptonite and survive, we can appreciate flying on a whole new level. What I mean is, we can know what it feels like to fly, to feel so good and be so joyful that we simply feel ah-mazing.

Don't get me wrong. You don't have to have a serious issue to understand the value of feeling amazing in your own skin. Just having the flu, or a stomach bug, or a broken toe, or a sprained ankle, can provide more than enough clarity for you to value good health. But so can escaping the trap of aging. In fact, aging may be one of the greatest teachers of all when it comes to appreciating the value of good health. But aging may also be the greatest enemy of good health as it is almost like a ninja assassin. At least with acute injury or sickness, you can have immediate clarity. But with aging, it drips in. It sneaks up on you and even lies to you. It is slow, and you may believe it is a necessity, something that "happens to us all," so you may decide to accept it as your fate rather than search out the truth of its relevance toward your health.

Anyway, the point is kryptonite is Superman's weakness. It makes him physically vulnerable. Being physically vulnerable can give birth to mental and emotional pain and weakness. If Superman were real, it would be easy to imagine that the first encounter with kryptonite would cause a great mental and emotional "cross to bear." After all, coming to terms with one's physical vulnerability or one's physical limits can be quite heavy.

I know, I know. Superman always recovers. Unlike the rest of us, for Superman, the pain caused by kryptonite never injures his soul because that is the way he was created. What I mean is that when Superman was imagined, he wasn't created to *know* pain. I'm not saying he wasn't created to experience pain; I'm saying he wasn't created to *know* it or to be intimate with it. He doesn't dwell on his injuries or past illnesses. He doesn't know how to age either, and he certainly never seems to dwell on it. My point is that Superman only knows how to fly, to rise again and again. That's the essence of his being. He only knows courage, willingness, and compassion. He's never afraid, so he never dwells on fear. And that's how he always recovers.

Yes, I'm talking about a fictional character who was designed to be perfect. But it has been my experience that all fiction comes from nonfiction. What is imagined comes from what is. The beauty and strength of Superman, or Wonder Woman, comes from the beauty and strength that is actually within each and every one of us. We are the nonfiction that brought about these fictional heroes. They are us. Or we are them.

We are designed to feel amazing in our bodies, to feel so good in our minds and bodies that we can't help but feel as if we could fly much like the superheroes we have created. There was a time when most of us felt this way, when most of us felt this amazing. It was when we were young.

I understand that some of us have suffered tragedy at a very young age. Pain and fear can embed themselves in a young child. But for most of us, as children, we spent our days feeling quite amazing; we radiated light, we laughed, we played, we explored, we were curious. We didn't know to be afraid of things. We had to be taught to be afraid, and until that happened, we didn't even know how to dwell on negative things because we didn't think all that much. We spent our days with an open mind and a free body. In other words, there was a time when feeling amazing was our default operational state.

If it were our default operational state, that means it still is. That's really what this book is about—returning to the original you or rediscovering the you(th) that you once enjoyed.

The truth is, we've all been exposed to a form of kryptonite, false information. We've all been told things, we've all accepted things, and we've even experienced things that we believe to be the truth about ourselves, our bodies, our condition, and our potential. Yet all of us, if we look around, can find those few people who seem to radiate life and vitality throughout their entire lives. These are the people who don't seem to age; it's as if they still believe they can fly.

Are they special? Do they have better genetics? Or have they simply tapped into something the rest of us don't seem to know anything about? No, to all of these questions. More than likely, these outliers have simply not lost sight as to who they really are. They haven't lost themselves.

Many of us have lost our original selves. We've forgotten how we started out in this life; how we were filled with joy, boundless energy, curiosity, tenacity, and grit. There was a time when we didn't know that we couldn't fly. There was a time when we were not bound by the thoughts of others, or worse, the thoughts of ourselves.

We are the reason we age. We are the reason we don't feel good. Or, to say it more pleasantly, we hold the keys to feeling young again. We can return to our original selves.

We are meant to know how to fly, to feel amazing throughout our lives. We were all created for an abundant life full of overflowing strength, energy, and joy. This is the life most of us all experienced before we started conforming to this world and its ways.

If this resonates with you, there is a reason for that. This book is for you. But if this sounds like nonsense to you, yet you wish it were true, keep reading a little further. You might discover something you thought you had lost.

I AM

Being a superhero may not resonate with you, but I know feeling good does. One thing I've learned from being a personal trainer for the last twenty-two years is that everyone wants to feel good. No matter what they tell you, what they are really saying is, "I want to feel good."

"I want to lose weight." = "I don't feel good in my body."

"I want more energy." = "I wish I felt better."

"I want bigger muscles." = "I want to feel good about myself."

"I want to move better." = "I want to feel good and be free in my body."

Do you see what I mean? Regardless of what a person wants to change about themselves, the real underlying reason is they want to feel good again.

Again.

That word is important. Do you know when most everyone feels amazing? When they are young. Do you know when people start not feeling amazing? When they put away the ways of a child and start believing they've lost their youth. Youth is the elixir that gives us the ah-mazing feeling in our bodies. Age is the lie that robs it. Or at least age is the lie that, if we believe it, robs our youth.

Do you remember what it was like to be a child? Do you remember the life you were able to enjoy? You were fearless. You climbed things, jumped off those things, maybe you dug holes in the yard, or built sandcastles, played with ladybugs, caught lightning bugs, you laughed and giggled most all the time, and you likely woke up with a smile on your face. Don't you remember how much life poured out of you when you were young? If not, do you see that life ooze out of your kids, your grandkids, or your neighbor's kids? The youth and exuberance of a child is the expression of the life force inside that child. It's beautiful to witness. It's amazing to feel.

Ponder these questions: Can the life force that is being expressed in a child grow weary with age? Or, can the spark of life that animates you grow dim? What if one of the reasons people didn't feel good as adults is because they invited another alternative into their thoughts and beliefs? What if they allowed their faith in aging to override or set aside the youth, strength, and joy that was always meant to flow from them?

I'm not saying we don't grow older. I'm saying maybe we aren't meant to grow weary and break down with age. After all, old lions still roar. Old eagles still fly until they die. They do this because they don't know any alternatives. The life that is in them is always expressed in its beauty until they expire. But with humans, it's a bit different. We get stuck in the idea of being human with all the limitations that it brings, and we lose focus on the truth that we are human *beings*. It's the *being* part that is limitless. It's the *being* part of us that we lose sight of. It is the *being* part of us that does not age. Unless we tell it to…

Am is a verb of *being*. Am is how we describe our being.

"I am." That statement is powerful because it yields the power to create. We create what we place after the "am."

"I am strong." Darn right, you are.

"I am weak." Yes, probably so.

"I am old." You are now.

"I am forever young." Preach it!

"I am." Now we are talking limitless potential!

If we don't add to the "am," we are full of infinite potential. When we add to the "am," we aim the potential and give it direction through the declaration.

If you think this is crazy, it's not. The body follows the head (the heart). What you believe and think about your "am-ness" determines the direction your body and your outcome will go. You know this is true, and you see this very thing play out in your life and the lives around you wherever you go.

This is what is meant by Proverbs 4:23:

"Guard your heart above all else, for it determines the course of your life." - NLT

"Keep your heart with all diligence, for out of it springs the issues of life." - NKJV

Your "am-ness" is your heart. You have to protect your "am." What you attach to or bury inside your "am," your *being*, determines the path you will take.

This idea has so much depth, please don't miss it. But to keep it simple, if you don't want to be old and weary, or weak and fragile, don't go around attaching those thoughts and beliefs to your being.

Your "am" follows what you attach to it.

You are *strong*.

You are *youth*.

You are *vitality*.

You *are*.

Using What You Have

To understand a thing, all you have to do is follow the design of a thing. Let's take a look at your design.

You are born pre-programmed to be strong and joyful. You have an original operating program—the developmental sequence that executes and instructs your growth and development. Once it starts running, this program constantly feeds and builds on itself, building you. The more it makes you move, the more you learn how to move; the more you learn how to move, the more you can move. All along the way through this directed and collected movement, you build, reinforce, and establish your nervous system and your "you-ness." The point is you are born with an original operating program designed to make you and keep you strong, healthy, and joyful.

And that is the point. You have a program designed to build you and keep you strong. What you do not have is a program designed to run at a certain time that begins to tear you down and age you out. You are not pre-programmed with an aging, weakening, fading software. If you have such a program, it did not come with your design. It is an addition you have made or a perversion of your original software. And just in case you're computer savvy, you may be thinking that the issue of age and breakdown must be a hardware issue. But that doesn't really fly because your hardware is alive, and it simply does what the internal operating system tells it to do with the resources that you provide it.

Following the design of the internal operating system and providing the body with good quality resources, we should be able to live a life of vitality at any age. That is our design; to live a life with strength, to have youth and vitality throughout all your many trips and cycles around the sun. In fact, what we consider the "prime of life" is really only the beginning third of life. There is much more life left to live after this so-called "prime." What is the point of ramping up with strength, energy, and vitality from years 0–20 only to decline and waste away from years 21–100? Just looking at the skew of those numbers should paint a picture of truth.

If that's the case, you may be asking yourself, "Where does our youth go then?" or "Why do I feel like I'm old?" Or, you may simply be balking and thinking, "Yeah, right. I'm not young anymore. I'm old and tired, and I simply can't do what I once could."

You're already aware of what I think about attaching directions and directives to your "am," but let's chase some different trains of thought here.

What if your experience, or what you believe about your youth, is not the whole story? What if what you are experiencing is simply what you are accepting or expecting? What if you easily settled for the common stories of the world? Or, what if the reason you aren't young anymore is that you stopped using your youth? What if you have simply succumbed to the governing law of "use it or lose it?" What if you really haven't lost your youth at all, but you've shelved it or traded it out?

What I mean is, what if you couldn't lose what was given to you and intended for you to keep? That would be tragic, wouldn't it? To think you had lost your youth, or that you must grow old and weary because that's the "course of nature" when the only reason this has become your experience is because you accepted a false notion.

Whatever your thoughts about youth, or your present experience about it, you can't lose what's not yours to lose. I'm not saying you can't shelve it or misplace it, but I am saying you can't lose it. Your youth, your strength and vigor, is in your design, and it will remain in your design until you end your many sun cycles, no matter how many trips you end up making.

I know it sounds like I'm crazy, but what if…what if I'm not wrong? What if the secret to youth was "hidden" inside your design, inside of you, and it is always there waiting to be used or tapped into? Would you be curious enough to look?

Since the beginning of time, man has looked for ways to rediscover his youth. The quest for the Fountain of Youth has always been playing out in some shape or form. Whether it involved rituals, long voyages in ships to faraway lands, or trying to manipulate hormones, man has continuously sought what has always been within his grasp.

You know the old saying, "It's always the last place you look." As far as your youth is concerned, it may be in the place that you've never looked—inside of yourself. Hear me out. Looking for the Fountain of Youth is like looking all over your house for your car keys only to feel like an idiot when you discover that you've been holding them in your hands the whole time. But you've done that, so you know it's possible. What if it was possible to hold your youth but misplace it in the same way, just like your keys? What if you simply had to become aware that you were already holding it, that it's in your grasp waiting to be realized and then used, just like your set of car keys?

I do believe it's possible for us to restore our youth, hold on to it, or rediscover it. I'm not alone in this thought, either. There have been a few throughout the centuries who have discovered the secret ways of youth. From Moses to Tibetan Monks to ageless yogis and gurus, there have been those who knew where to find their youth and how to keep it. These are the ones who knew they could not find what was in them by looking outside of themselves. Or, maybe they just didn't believe they could ever lose what was theirs to keep. Maybe they didn't think youth was a vapor to fade away but an energy to be used. And, if there is any truth to the governing law of "use it or lose it," what if they were just simply wise enough to use their youth so they could keep it?

The point is, there is a great deal of wonder placed inside of our design. We have been given many gifts that we were all intended to use. I believe youth is one of those gifts. It's ours to use, and it's inside all of us. We just have to engage in it again.

Before we get too deep in our design, let's take a look at the truth behind some of the legends of youth.

THE TRUTH BEHIND LEGENDS

Throughout all of history, there have been fantastic tales of those who never aged, and there have been fantastic voyages of those in search of their secret. Regardless of the culture, or the time, all of humankind has cherished and sought the secret of youth.

In the Bible, there are tales of those like Methuselah, who lived to be 969 years old. Of course, if that's hard to swallow or fathom, it is said that after the great flood man's years were considerably shortened. Moses is said to have lived to be 120 years old and that when he died, he died with the strength of a young man and the vision of an eagle. That may sound hard to imagine, but today's science and research suggests that Moses's story is actually plausible and that humans are able to live between 115 to 120-something years old. In modern times we do have people making it along that far.

I know, who wants to live to be 123 years old and have to live in a rest home for 40 of those years? No one. What's the point of living over a hundred years if you are imprisoned in your own broken, weak body? That would be hell. But it seems that those small few who make it well past 100 years of age still enjoy a great quality of life and they still employ the use of their sharp minds and able bodies.

You've probably heard the stories like I have, about a few Yogis who live to be well over a hundred years old and yet they still practice yoga, they still smile, and they still regularly outperform people less than half their age.

Are these stories true?

It does appear they are. Swami Buaji was said to be 116 years old with the anatomical age of a 40-year-old[1]. At 116 years of age, he had perfect eyesight, full strength, and stamina, and he was still teaching students how to perform and engage in yoga. He was full of life. Yes, he looked "mature" in age, but his vitality flowed from him with ferocity. What secret did this man know? Was he simply practicing movements seen as yoga, or was he also practicing and living from a deeper well of knowledge beyond the movements? Like the life of Moses, Swami Buaji's life is evidence that it is possible to maintain the youth and strength of a young man with the longevity of a tortoise.

But Swami Buaji is just one example. Other disciplines, like those in the martial arts, exhibit ageless masters as well. Lu Zijian, a Qigong master, reached the age of 118 years "full of vigor and a bright spirit."[2] He obviously knew something about youth and longevity. Was it his discipline of movement, his practice of Taoism, or both? Or something more?

Swami Buaji and Lu Zijian are evidence that what was said about Moses is possible for us as well. These recently living legends point to our potential. They are not

---

[1] https://www.huffpost.com/entry/swami-buaji-116-yogi_b_851710?guccounter=1
[2] http://luzijian.com/

exceptions or outliers as much as they are examples of the way things should be, and they are certainly examples of the way things can be.

It is said that Swami and Lu were both kind, gracious, and gentle, and that both of them spent their lives in the service of others. Maybe that was the secret to their vitality. Could it be that having a purpose driven by love is what keeps a person young in spirit and able in body?

The Fountain of Youth

Tales of the Fountain of Youth have also been around throughout all of history. As I child, I first learned of the quest for the Fountain of Youth in grade school when we were studying world explorers. At that time, it was said that Ponce De Leon discovered Florida while he was looking for the Fountain of Youth. The Healing Hole of Bimini in the Bahamas is said to be the actual waters that Ponce de Leon was searching for.

It's funny how sometimes history changes itself. Most historians today think that Ponce de Leon's search for the Fountain of Youth was a myth, that he wasn't looking for such a fountain, but he was more interested in conquering lands and acquiring gold. But I'm not so sure about that. There is always truth behind legend. Besides, if he was a conquistador and conquest and gold were on his grocery list, possessing water that heals and restores youth would bring more wealth than all the gold in the world. After all, gold won't make you happy, unless of course, you could use it to buy youth.

The search for healing waters has been laced throughout history in all cultures. My town, Fuquay-Varina, was established over the search for waters that heal. I'm not joking about the name of my town or its history. In 1805, a Frenchman named William Fuquay purchased the land in my town, and his family discovered a mineral spring that seemed to possess healing properties. People traveled from far and wide to participate in the "taking of the waters" to restore their health. The attraction to the mineral spring was so great that it helped give birth to my town, due to all the people voyaging in search of their youth.

There is even a legend of a conversation in the Bible between a lady at a well and a passerby who began discussing waters that heal.

> *"Everyone who drinks this water will be thirsty again, but whoever drinks the water I give them will never thirst. Indeed, the water I give them will become in them a spring of water welling up to eternal life." The woman said to him, "Sir, give me this water so that I won't get thirsty and have to keep coming here to draw water." - John 4:13-15*

If you follow the above passage, the gentleman is telling the lady that the healing waters come from inside, not out in the world. He's telling her life and vitality come from within.

We are all looking for the same thing: life. Life being vitality, vigor, youth, and strength. It's all the same thing. It's the stuff that legends are made of, the stuff that causes the miraculous growth of an oddly named town and the stuff that causes deeper conversations with a complete stranger at a well. We all want life, and we are willing to look anywhere for it or talk to anyone to get it.

But perhaps the gentleman in the story above was right? What if everything we want—our youth, health, strength, and joy—is waiting for us inside our very design? Could the Fountain of Youth be in us already? Maybe so. After all, it is a pretty miraculous design. We draw out of it what we put into it.

THE MIRACULOUS MACHINE

"We are shaped by our thoughts; we become what we think." - Buddha

Every day of your life, starting from birth, your body has taken in information and then somehow created an outcome (you). You are the accumulation and the expression of all the information your nervous system receives. Our brains are information junkies; they can't get enough information. And from that information, our brains give out commands and functions, or "outformation."

Our outformation is our expression; how we move, how we think, how we feel, and even how we look. But this is a perpetual loop of information as our outformation also becomes our information, which in turn affects our expression, which in turn again becomes information.

Our bodies have a miraculous design. We are created from the inside out through a never-ending cycle or self-perpetuated input, or through self-perpetuated information. The better the information, the better the expression of who we are. We are "both/and" not "either/or" beings. What I mean is that nothing about us is separated from another part of us. Everything about us is connected, which means everything about us *is* information, and everything about us *is* expression. Every movement, every thought, every cell, every bite of food, every sensation, every observation, every breath, every emotion—it's all information. And from that information, it all becomes expression.

Throughout our lives, we express what we generate. If we want optimal expression—youth, strength, health, and vitality—then we have to generate optimal information. This is the key to longevity and feeling amazing, or having a body fit to live the adventure of life through all the decades we enter into. We must provide our brains with optimal information in as many areas as possible. This includes the information we receive and *perceive* from the outside world as well as the information we generate from within ourselves.

Take notice that I said we perceive the information we receive from the outside world. This would mean we actually generate all information we receive, and that may sound odd.

Yes, information can and does come to us, but our interpretation of this information is what gets relayed and expressed. Our interpretation becomes the input more than the actual input does. Our interpretation of wind, smells, tone, inflection, touch—they are all sensory-driven and interpreted. This gets really complicated, but the point is, we are expressions of all the information we generate. And if we want certain outcomes, we need to provide certain information.

In the most oversimplified explanation I can provide, if you want to be young, you cannot be thinking "old." We are what we do, how we feel, how we think, what we eat, and how we breathe. We are living miracle machines. We create and express what we plant.

You've heard this before, I think. If you've ever read any of my books, somewhere in each of them, I refer to the "use it or lose it" principle. The body prunes away things it does not use. Another way to look at this is that the body does not produce what is not planted. We lose things because we don't use things.

Basically, we can't express what we want to have if we don't plant the information we need. Our body will not yield the "crops" we want to harvest if we don't sow certain seeds of information.

If we want something, we have to sow it inside of our miraculous design. We do this by using what we have been given or challenging what we want to express through thoughts and physical attempts to express it. We have to use what we want to have or generate the information we need in order to have what we desire.

This means the "use it or lose it" principle could also be seen as the "use it and have it" principle. Again, it's all about the input and then information we sow or generate.

Our impressions determine our expressions.

Our input determines our output.

Our income determines our outcome.

Our inside determines our outside.

What we plant, we reap.

Food, thoughts, emotions, movement—it's all input, it's all information. And the input can be multiplied and compounded. For example, the quality of food we eat determines how our body will function and carry out its processes. But our thoughts about that food, or our body, or that argument we just had right before we eat, can compound the input of the food in a greater way. I'll talk more about this later, but basically, different inputs can come together for better or for worse when it comes to the outcome or the expression.

If you think this is confusing, all you need to know is that you are a creator. You create your experiences and expressions. You also create your state of being. You do this by honoring or ignoring your design. By embracing it or neglecting it. Through intention or apathy. However you look at it, you are the creator in your story and if you want to live a long life of youth and strength, you can. The easiest way to enjoy longevity is to use your design—just like you did when you were a child.

The Origin of Longevity

As I said before, we were all born with an original operating program embedded in our nervous system. This original program has one major operative and command for the body: move and become. The program drives the body to move through reflexes, and these reflex-driven movements stimulate the growth of the nervous system and, ultimately, the growth of the body and all its abilities.

This movement-driven design feeds itself like a snowball rolling down a hill. The smallest movements help create growth and production of neural connections in the brain and throughout the nervous system. The more these new neural connections are made, the more this neural wiring takes place, the more the body can move. As the body moves, it acquires stability, mobility, control, and strength. These qualities of expression become more and more refined as the body moves. It takes movement to build and grow the nervous system and connect the brain. As the nervous system grows and becomes efficient, the body's capability of movement increases, feeding more growth in the nervous system. It's a wonderful cycle—perhaps the true circle of life.

This growth that is started from the hardwired operating program builds more than the nervous system and the body. It also develops the mind and matures the emotions. As the body moves according to the operating program, it connects the brain, allowing it to achieve higher levels of reasoning, focus, attention, creativity, and thought. It also allows the brain and mind to experience the wonderful emotions of joy and peace. The better the body moves, the better the emotions. This is also circular. The better the emotions, the better they can be understood and controlled, the better the body moves.

All of this growth, all of this ability, is driven through the simplest reflexes and from the smallest movements. The body is designed in such a way that movement is the vehicle for the growth of the whole person: body, mind, and emotions. The design is intended to be self-perpetuating. Once it starts, the growth and maintenance of the body is intended to continue throughout life. Understand this: the body's ability to creatively and freely express itself in controlled movement, thought, and emotion is intended through its design. As long as we move according to the design, according to the initial hardwired movement program, we *should* be able to maintain our youth and vigor.

Driven by reflexive movement, the initial movement program carries the body through a series of movement stages. We call this the developmental sequence. This sequence lays the foundation for all the creative expression (movement and thought) potential you have. Throughout your entire life, regardless of your age, these foundational movement stages can be revisited and constantly reinforced.

There are three pillars of human movement. These three pillars help establish our "am-ness." They are our movement foundation, and they are essential for us to enjoy a life of strength, health, and longevity. These three pillars are hardwired in each of us, and they automatically began once we were born. They are embedded in and woven throughout the developmental sequence. As we age and mature, however, these three pillars become more of a choice and less of a drive. While we are programmed with them and designed to carry them out at all times, they may end up competing with habits, thoughts, stress, and other learned issues of life. It's important to understand that just because we choose not to do them doesn't mean we are not designed to do them in every moment of our lives.

Let's look at these three pillars, *the movement foundation* of all we can be, and all we can enjoy here on this earth in this life.

The Three Pillars of Human Movement

Pillar #1: The Breath of Life

No avalanche is possible without the first snowflake. Think about it. The landscape changing, destructive power that is expressed during an avalanche would not be possible without the gentleness of the first fallen snowflake. Like an avalanche, the human body is limitless in its expressive potential, but none of that potential would be possible without the gentleness of a functional diaphragmatic breath.

It is the first breath we take that begins the foundation for all that we are. It is the last breath we take that will put a period at the end of our story. We are born to be belly breathers; we are meant to fill our lungs from the bottom to the top. A functional diaphragmatic breath is the foundation for power and life-lasting youth.

When we enter the world, we are nasal breathers. We breathe in and out through our nose, and we fill our lungs from the bottom to the top. As we grow and develop, we begin to learn other breathing strategies, either through necessity, life events, or choice. These other strategies do not highlight a flaw in our design but point to the beauty of our design because we are designed to both thrive and survive.

To thrive, we have an originally intended way of being—in this case, a diaphragmatic breath. To survive, we develop numerous strategies to ensure we have a body to be in (to prevent the body from dying). One such strategy would be breathing through our mouths, using the emergency breathing muscles of the neck and chest. Surviving to see another day is great! These surviving strategies the body has can indeed be life-saving. The only issue with surviving is that surviving is to be short-lived; we are designed to return to thriving. But many of us don't. Many of us get stuck in the surviving mode, in the compensatory or life-saving strategy mode. Life stuck in surviving mode leads to becoming "old" or "breaking down" with time.

The body is made to thrive. Thriving is where youth and longevity are found, even at age 110. The only way to thrive and feel amazing throughout life is to maintain our default way of breathing, gently filling the lungs from the bottom to the top. Notice, I said "gently."

Strength is gentle. I mean, real strength is established on a proper functional diaphragmatic breath. This breath is soft and fluid. There is a flow to it. When one breathes as they were designed, their neck is soft, their shoulders are relaxed, their posture is erect, and they move with fluid ease. By contrast, a compensatory breath, an emergency breath, can be sharp and forceful, or weak, rapid, and shallow. When one breathes using a dysfunctional breathing pattern (an alternate breathing strategy), the chest and shoulders often lift sharply and fall sharply. The neck bulges, the head often protrudes forward, their posture is less than optimal, and their movements are stiff and disjointed.

A life spent properly breathing is a life full of lasting vitality. A life spent in emergency breathing is a life full of stress, anxiety, inflammation, wear, and tear. Emergency breathing leads to decay and breakdown at an accelerated rate.

Is it Safe?

Have you ever seen the movie *Marathon Man*? There is a painful scene where a Nazi dentist is interrogating Dustin Hoffman by drilling into his teeth without any anesthetics. The Nazi's question to Hoffman's character was, "Is it safe?" Over and over again, he would ask this question, and depending on the answer, he would drill into Hoffman's teeth. That would certainly be torture. Not entirely like this investigation of torture, our nervous system is constantly asking this same question: "Is it safe?"

The answer to this question is found in every breath we take. A proper, functional diaphragmatic breath says, "Yes. It is safe." A breath taken using the emergency breathing muscles says, "Incoming, sound the alarms! It is NOT safe!" A life spent breathing up in the neck and chest says, "Don't go outside, ever. Stay in the bomb shelter. It's too dangerous out there."

The nervous system wants to be safe. If it feels safe, it will allow us to thrive. If it feels threatened, it will ensure we survive. As an analogy, I think a sea anemone is perhaps the greatest picture of how our nervous system operates. Sea anemones are like beautiful flowing flowers in the ocean. They dance in the current of the water—if they feel safe. Once a threat is perceived, they withdraw, shrink, and close up to protect themselves. In other words, once they are threatened, they seek survival and withdraw their beauty. But when there is no longer a threat, once they determine it is safe again, they open up and flow in the current; they express their beauty with the world again. That is how our nervous system operates.

When it feels safe, it allows us to thrive, to fully and freely express ourselves without limitations. Without limitations for us would mean full expression in mobility, strength, fluidity, thought, creativity, and so on. But when the nervous system doesn't feel safe, when it is determining there is a threat, when our very breath screams, "Sound the alarms!" it puts the brakes on our ability to express ourselves. When the alarms sound, adrenaline and cortisol (our stress hormones) are released, and our muscles stiffen for a fight or a frantic flee. Our emotions also get an "edge." Our inputs get heightened or exaggerated as all incoming stimulus is now under "safety scrutiny." And our thoughts become laced with survival tactics like suspicion, anger, and doubt, which in turn brings our thoughts to confusion and illusion, spiraling into false stories that we end up telling ourselves about ourselves or others. This now grows into a nightmare because our thoughts are more input to the nervous system, ringing the alarm bells louder and louder until we just spiral out of control and end up in a perpetual "IT IS NEVER SAFE!" mode. We spend our entire life in aches, pains, stiffness, fear, bitterness, anger, and distrust.

Whoa—this gets crazy. But it happens ALL THE TIME. The good news is this can all be stopped. It can all be surrendered and returned to "GOOD" with one gentle, functional breath of design. Our life, our happiness, our strength, and our longevity all rest in the message of a simple breath: "It is safe."

How can we best ensure that we can provide our nervous system with this reassuring message it longs to hear? We simply return to our default way of breathing:

- Keep your tongue rested on the roof of your mouth
    - If you don't know where that is, just swallow and attend to where your tongue goes. That's the place of rest for the tongue.

- Keep your lips closed, but relaxed
- Breathe in and out through your nose
- Fill your lungs from the bottom to the top (belly first, then chest)

This is the original default way of breathing. This is the "I am safe, I am strong" way of breathing. Breathing like this can calm emotions and settle out-of-control thoughts (inputs that always yield less than desired outputs). The natural breath is where youth and longevity are found and enjoyed throughout life. It is truly the breath of life.

Pillar #2: The Balance of It All

The second Pillar of Human Movement is activating the vestibular system. An overly simplified, but appropriate explanation of the vestibular system would be to say it is our balancing system. Without balance, we can have no real life worth living. This is true in our bodies and our outer experiences.

Physically, a healthy vestibular system, a healthy "balance" system, is a necessity for living a strong life of longevity. A life out of balance soon burns out or wears out quickly. This is also true for the body. In the body, having balance or a healthy vestibular system is essential for having the ability to move well with strength and ease throughout life. It is also essential for having a mind capable of free, fluid thought that can rule its emotions rather than be ruled by them.

The balance system (the vestibular system) is found inside the head, behind the ears. One of its key functions is to keep the head level with the horizon. Every single muscle in the body is reflexively connected to the vestibular system to proactively and reactively ensure that the head can always maintain this position—it's a matter of health and survival.

Another key function of the vestibular system is that it is the collection agency—or funnel—for ALL incoming information generated and received by the body. All roads of sensory input and all other roads of input deep below consciousness flow through the vestibular system to be imported into the brain. The healthier the vestibular system is, the healthier and more complete this information collection process is. Think about it. A balance system that collects all the data there is to know about the world may easily corrupt that incoming data if the balance system itself is out of alignment. If all of this incoming data is going to be used to optimally command the body's responses for millions of simultaneous processes, the vestibular system itself has to be *in balance*.

There is inherent wisdom inside the body. Remember, the nervous system wants to feel safe. If the vestibular system isn't healthy, the nervous system will not feel safe—it knows. As a consequence, every commanded response or expression given out by the brain to the body will be a command aimed at survival. Years of commanded responses aimed at survival, due to a vestibular system out of balance, never allow the body to rest. Without rest, the body cannot thrive. This means youth, health, and vigor cannot be maintained. A lifetime spent in survival mode breaks the body down and robs its youth. The vestibular system must be healthy for the body to thrive.

The key to having a healthy vestibular system is to actively use it or engage in it. This is the key to everything about the body's design. Remember, use it to have it.

Let's consider the design.

The vestibular system will try to keep the head on the horizon at all possible costs, and the vestibular system will collect all the information it can from the body to ensure the head can always return to and maintain this position.

Also, note where the vestibular system is found: in the head on top of an amazing swivel that can flex, extend, and rotate in every possible plane of motion. The vestibular system sits on top of this "super swivel" in order to command the body to right the head on the horizon. The vestibular system is kept healthy and robust through the constant use of this super swivel (the neck) along with the constant incoming information provided by the body.

In other words, all we have to do to keep a healthy vestibular system is to move our heads often and move our bodies throughout the day. This seems ridiculously simple, I know, but consider how our modern society has made it possible to spend most of our lives with little to no head movement and minimal body movement. Now consider the energy and the movement of young, happy children. They are constantly moving and balancing their heads while they run, jump, flip, and play. They are robust and overflowing with life—the kind of life that comes from a light deep within them. It's beautiful.

Until you put a smartphone or tablet into their hands. What happens then? They age. Their heads get held down, fixed in one position, their eyes no longer scan the horizon for the joys of the world, their bodies no longer leap, bound, and skip, but instead, they learn how to sit and fix all their attention on an entertainment device. They learn to use their heads held down, and their bodies follow this information. Their thoughts and emotions also bow down to this constant, never-changing information. Eventually, the wonder of their design submits to the new use it has found. The design learns that it is no longer needed to leap and bound and roll and play or squeal with delight from the eyes. So it folds and gives in to the demand of how it is being used and youth fades away, even in the young.

Know this: youth is not lost in age, but in disengagement. Youth must be used to be enjoyed. It's all use it to have it. It's all balance. If you want youth throughout your many years, you must engage in your design. There is no need to thrive with robust vigor if all you do is sit with your head fixed in one spot while your body remains in one place. Once the nervous system removes the neural connections that were kept for optimal life experience, the remaining neural connections will be those needed to maintain survival. If the nervous system is trying to maintain survival, it does not feel safe. If the nervous system does not feel safe, it strives to survive, and then the freedom of physical and mental expression, the energy and vibrancy of youth, and the strength of life fade away. Growing old happens when we stop moving.

Not moving tells the nervous system we don't need to move. The nervous system takes action to make this new demand possible and efficient by removing neural pathways that are no longer being used. When we no longer move, we are neglecting the wonderful infrastructure designed to allow us to move so the nervous system prunes it away. We don't need it, so we shed it. But life is funny; we may actually need to move at times. Moving without the proper neural infrastructure is risky. It threatens the safety of the nervous system, which further locks us down and restricts us from moving and feeling well, making us feel "old" or "weak" or "fragile."

How do we reverse this process and return to our youth? We engage in our design and create the need for those neural connections we once pruned away. If we create the need regularly, the nervous system will respond and begin to regenerate itself, restoring our strength, our vigor, our energy, and even our creativity.

You cannot expect to feel amazing and youthful if you live in your handheld devices or spend all your time slouched in front of a screen. You must stimulate your vestibular system through movement—moving your eyes, your head, and your body. This is how you keep your vestibular system healthy and feed your brain with rich sensory information. This is where you maintain and balance your youth with your time here on Earth.

Pillar #3: The Secret of the X

Your body is an X. Not only are you shaped like an X, but you are also neurologically wired and physically connected or knit together like an X. Neurologically, the right side of your brain controls the left side of your body, and the left side of your brain controls the right side of your body. Physically, your left arm is connected to your right foot through a series of cross-connecting (more Xs) muscles, tendons, and fascia, and your right arm is connected to your left foot in the same way. These cross-connections act like energy transferring slings that propel you from one place to another. That is, when you walk, your right foot and left arm move forward and backward together as do your left foot and right arm. This motion generates and transfers energy efficiently through the center of your body. When your opposing limbs move rhythmically together, they flex and extend the slings that connect them, propelling you along effortlessly. They also provide rich nourishment to your brain, and this information keeps your brain very healthy and YOUNG.

The secret to a life of strength is found in this cross-lateral design. In other words, our gait pattern is intended to keep us healthy and strong throughout life. Crawling, walking, marching, skipping, running, sprinting—these are life-giving, youth-keeping movements, *if* they are carried out according to the original instructions of our internal operating system.

We are designed to walk with our arms. This is extremely evident when crawling but often forgotten while walking. And this is another area where youth fades away. We are designed to use all four limbs when we travel by self-propulsion. It has been said that the arms are like the engines of our body, our torso is like the transmission of our body, and our legs are like the wheels. It is our arms that drive us. If you want to see this truth in action, watch the arms of Olympic sprinters driving out of the starting blocks, or notice the use and action of their arms as they run the 100-meter dash. The arms move the body with power and efficiency.

Crawling makes the use of the arms evident as it is our most basic gait pattern, and sprinting highlights and exaggerates the use of our arms as it is our most explosive gait pattern. Considering the spectrum of our gait pattern, from crawling to sprinting, it should stand to reason that the arms are still intended to drive the body during our normal, most efficient gait pattern: walking.

Walking with our arms maintains our strength and gives us longevity. It does this because it helps keep the center of our X strong by exercising the slings that connect our opposing limbs. The coordinated opposing motion of our limbs also helps the torso to maintain control as it *efficiently* mitigates the rotational forces created by the limbs swinging back and forth.

Notice the word *efficiently*. This is also where longevity comes in. There is an energy cost to not walking or running as we are designed to walk or run. It takes more energy for the body to walk and run if it is not using the arms to counter the swing of the legs because the body cannot take advantage of the slings that connect the opposing limbs. More energy spent moving the body with compensation strategies means more "wear and tear" on the body. Walking without the arms ushers the body to expend more energy, and it hastens the aging process as it places undue wear on parts of the body that should never wear out if the body is moving optimally.

Perhaps the biggest youth secret found in our X is the effect that walking with our arms has on the brain. Imagine that your brain is divided into two halves—a right half and a left half. Now imagine that a canyon or a great divide is separating the two halves. Engaging in our true gait pattern, using all four limbs, connects the two halves of the brain by establishing "neural bridges" across the great divide. From crawling to walking, the more we engage in these contralateral patterns, the more neural bridges we create and establish between the two hemispheres. The more neural bridges that are built and established between the two halves, the better the transfer of information, the better the communication and coordination between the two halves. This results in a whole, connected, and efficient brain. An efficient and connected brain is a youthful and capable brain. It can process thoughts, control emotions, solve problems, create beauty, and move the body like poetry. If there were a movement that was intended to keep us young and healthy forever, it would be walking.

Not only does walking with the arms connect the brain and makes it whole, but it may also protect the brain from neurological diseases and disorders like Alzheimer's or dementia. It may even help combat neurological diseases like Parkinson's and multiple sclerosis. Neurological diseases erode the nervous system. Walking builds the nervous system. If you ever doubt that, just watch a growing and developing child. Movement (crawling and learning to walk) is their vehicle for growth, learning, and development. It's our vehicle too.

To summarize this section, there are Three Pillars of Human Movement:

1) Breathe properly with the diaphragm (fill the lungs from the bottom to the top)

2) Activate the vestibular system (use the head)
3) Engage in the true gait pattern (use the arms)

And woven in these three pillars and everything else you do, keep your tongue where it belongs—on the roof of your mouth.

The body is a miraculous design. Inside, it holds the keys to youth, longevity, strength, and health. We can never lose our original operating program, our original growth and development program. And, we simply do not have a decay, weakness, or fragility program. We have a design that offers a constant invitation to be used. To use it (to engage in it) fulfills its purpose—it knows it is needed. To neglect it is like saying, "I don't need or want you anymore," and this results in our bodies fading away. Youth is not wasted on the young, it's just wasted.

Fortunately, all is not lost forever. Even if you neglect your youth or misplace it, you can get a great deal of it back. Engaging in the three pillars of human movement creates a demand on the body. When a stress, a request, or a demand is placed on the body, it responds by building and reestablishing neural pathways in the brain. What was once pruned away can be grown again. It may take time to reestablish these pathways, but it took a few years to establish them the first time you built them. So it's okay if it takes a few months or more to get them back.

The important thing is that you can get them back! Just keep asking the body for them by engaging in your design often. I am going to lay out a simple plan to help you do this in a few chapters. It's easy to implement, and the rewards are life-changing, if not life-giving. But first, we need to talk about some other sources of information that enter into our nervous system.

THE OTHER MAJOR SOURCES OF INFORMATION

Remember that the body expresses itself based on the information that it is receiving. The input always determines the output, and this is a cyclical, never-ending dance between give and take. Movement, as programmed in your original operating system, is what gets this dance of being started. Our very first movements supply the needed information to develop our nervous systems and our bodies. And as long as we engage in our design, the Three Pillars of Human Movement (really, the Three Pillars of Human *Being*), we have the greatest chance of always supplying optimal information to our brains so that we can enjoy optimal expression.

It's almost that simple. But this is where it gets a little complicated. Everything matters, and everything becomes information. As we grow and develop, we become more able to acquire more and more information, and consequently, we become more able to express ourselves in an endless variety of ways; we develop habits, we accumulate knowledge, and we develop minds. Our personalities begin to develop and reveal themselves as well. As this happens, as we become who we are, we also gain the ability to start tinting or tainting the information we send to our brains.

As we grow and mature, the original movement program no longer provides the greatest source of input. It begins to compete with other sources of input and soon only provides the foundation or the framework for the information we generate. This brings me to the other major sources of input that greatly influence, enhance, tint, or pollute our dance of expression—the tongue, our food, our emotions, thoughts, beliefs, our conscious mind, and our unconscious mind.

Holding Your Tongue

Let's start with the tongue as it may be the easiest to conceptualize from a physical standpoint. From a movement perspective, the position of the tongue could be another Pillar of Human Movement. The more I have thought about it over the years, the more I've grown to think this may be the linchpin to the whole movement program. To be honest, in my head, "Three Pillars of Human Movement" sounds better than "Four Pillars of Human Movement." But that's just silly because four pillars could certainly support more structure than three.

Anyway, remember that the nervous system (the brain) craves information. And, based on the original movement template pre-programmed before birth, the brain is also expecting certain information to feel safe and complete. The position of the tongue is no exception to this, and it could be the greatest piece of the movement information puzzle that the brain is looking for to truly feel safe and free in order to express itself in its full potential.

It sounds ludicrous that something so simple and seemingly insignificant could matter in the grand scheme of your health and wellbeing, or even in your longevity, but it is often the smallest of things that yield the greatest of consequences or rewards. In the Bible, the tongue is described as the rudder that guides the whole ship. This is true on many levels. But physically, the tongue (your rudder) is what keeps the ship (your body) on the course to longevity, and it can also be used to make course corrections along the way.

It may help to think of the tongue as a light switch. If the switch is flipped down, the lights are off, and it makes it hard to see clearly. If the switch is flipped up, the lights are on, and all objects in the room are clearly seen. When you can clearly see, you move and navigate through a room freely; you can see, so you feel safe enough to move at will. When the lights are off, however, you move cautiously and slowly so you don't stump your toe, hit your knee on a corner, or smash your face into a wall. Likewise, when the tongue is "switched up" the information going to the brain is more whole and the nervous system can "see" more clearly. It feels safe. When the tongue is "switched down," the nervous system knows it is missing valuable information, so it guards itself through strategically placed restrictions.

You can test this out for yourself and know that it is true. So let's test it.

Place your feet together, straighten your knees, open your mouth, and place your tongue on the bottom of your mouth. Now try to touch your toes. Notice how it feels and how far you can reach. Now, close your mouth and place your tongue on the roof of your mouth and try to touch your toes again. How did that feel, and how far were you able to reach? Was there a change? Which way was better?

Likewise, you can do the same test with your breath. Open your mouth, place your tongue on the bottom of your mouth, and try to take a deep breath by inhaling through your nose. How did that feel? Now, close your mouth and place your tongue on the roof of your mouth and take a deep breath by inhaling through your nose. Was there a difference? Which way was easier?

The chances are great that you were able to breathe deeper and easier with your tongue on the roof of your mouth. This is because your tongue is neurologically connected to your diaphragm. But really, how could it not be? It's your tongue, inside your body, and everything about you matters. Nothing about you is insignificant.

Now extrapolate this new experiential knowledge and imagine how powerful tongue placement could be for your health taken breath by breath throughout your life. Keeping the tongue where it belongs helps to optimize every breath you take. But as you likely experienced in the toe touch, it also helps to optimize every movement you make as well.

Simply resting your tongue where it belongs makes everything better. It improves the way you breathe, it improves the way you move, and it even improves your posture. Resting your tongue during a conversation can even improve your relationships. That's "tongue in cheek" (get it?), but the truth is, keeping the tongue where it belongs makes your nervous system feel safe. A safe nervous system will provide space for better relationships as a safe nervous system is more apt to listen than to speak. Tongue placement could quite possibly be the greatest physical input (information) you can provide to your brain to ensure it always feels safe enough to allow you to freely express yourself and live a long life full of health and vigor in every possible way.

The Mind and Our Thoughts

And here is where everything gets deep. Our original operating movement program develops not just our bodies, but it also lays the physical framework to develop our minds. As our brain grows and becomes more efficient at processing information, it also begins to learn and acquire knowledge. Soon, with the knowledge we acquire, we begin to learn how to think, and we develop a personality. As we learn how to think, our very thoughts become information, and they also become physical neural connections in our brains. That's right, as we create thoughts, we create physical neural representations of those thoughts in our brains. Isn't that amazing? Thoughts are real.

Anyway, as we begin to think, choose, believe, and create, movement starts to become trumped as the major source of input for our nervous system. It's not that movement no longer generates all the wonderful information our nervous system wants, but this information can become "outweighed" by the depths of conscious and subconscious thoughts we begin to generate and collect.

What I'm trying to say is that our thoughts and beliefs can carry more weight in our nervous system than our movements do. Our thoughts and beliefs influence how we move. As far as our nervous system is concerned, our thoughts and beliefs—our conscious and unconscious minds—are always (at all times) giving the nervous system one of two messages:

1) I am safe.
2) I am not safe.

This is tricky. It's not that optimal movement no longer provides "safe" information to the nervous system, it's more that a negative thought can provide "unsafe" information to the nervous system, and this information, in turn, influences the expression of movement to where it becomes less than optimal. The good news is that a positive thought or truth can provide "safe" information to the nervous system and elevate or optimize the body's ability to move.

And yes, optimal movement can indeed elevate the thoughts and emotions as well, but optimal movement cannot and will never remove the thoughts and beliefs that are buried in the abyss of the heart (subconscious mind). Do you remember this truth mentioned above?

> *"Keep your heart with all diligence, for out of it springs the issues of life."* - Proverbs 4:23, NKJV

It's these issues that trump the design of movement and ultimately determine our expressions, our experiences, and our outcomes.

The DNA of the Soul

> *"The story in my mind controls me every time."*
> - Tim Epling

Our subconscious mind is like the genetic DNA of our soul. Just like our physical DNA orchestrates the function and purpose of our cells through our genetic code, the thoughts we keep buried in our hearts orchestrate the function and purpose of our lives through our "belief code." These buried beliefs are far below our conscious, mental radar, and they are always "on." They are always telling our nervous system a story of good and evil, right and wrong, or truth and lies. YOU don't recognize this, but your body does. What was created to be wild and free through movement becomes "protected," caged, and tamed through the ego. The ego protects us through its use of our mental framework of knowledge and beliefs. Ironically, the protection our ego offers us is what takes life away from us. That is, we no longer live with gusto and joy, but instead, we exist, we age, and we fade away.

This is why good movement cannot trump negative beliefs or buried thoughts. The beliefs and thoughts we keep in our heart impregnate every other source of information we generate. As a result, "the issues of life" express themselves through our bodies and our experiences.

This might seem a bit nebulous, so let's make this more practical by looking at some inputs we offer our bodies. Take broccoli, for example. Is broccoli "good" or "bad?" How you label it with your beliefs about it will determine how it affects you. But deeper than that still is how you label yourself. Are you "fat" or "weak" or "sickly?" Are you "ugly," "pretty," or "strong?" Will broccoli be "good" for you if you believe you are "fat?" Will it be "good" for you if you believe you are "strong?" There are layers to our thoughts, but the deepest thoughts, the roots of thought kept in our hearts, carry the greatest weight and influence our outcomes the most.

Buckle up because I'm going to pump the brakes on your mind right here: Under the right conditions, a chocolate chip cookie could be better for you than a carrot. If you eat a carrot in guilt, subconsciously thinking you are a lazy, fat slob, you are telling your nervous system a lie, and you are sending a signal that it is not safe. As a result, that would-be-good carrot cannot overcome the fight-or-flight response your subconscious mind is perpetually generating. The carrot cannot be adequately digested because your body is unsafe and is in survival mode. The carrot's nutrients cannot all be properly utilized. It may even cause gastrointestinal distress that leads to inflammation and anxiety or worse. How can a simple carrot benefit you through all the negative lies held in your subconscious mind? It would have to be a miracle carrot.

But let's consider a chocolate chip cookie. Is it good or bad for you? What if you ate a chocolate chip cookie in full joy without any guilt or thoughts of sabotage? What if you held the truth about yourself in your subconscious mind? If you ate a cookie subconsciously knowing that you were awesome, you were strong, and you were healthy, that cookie could really benefit you. If you know the truth about who you are, your nervous system is going to feel safe. It will allow your body to rest and digest, to thrive. Your body will be able to glean any available nutrients from that cookie without causing inflammation or distress to your system.

I'm not saying that there are no nutritional differences in foods, nor am I saying we should not be mindful of what we eat. I'm suggesting that how we label foods (and more importantly, how we label ourselves) is a greater determinant factor in the use and outcome of the food we eat. In other words, don't just be mindful of what you eat, be mindful of *how* you eat and the thoughts you keep within yourself.

Nutrition is a very sticky subject, so just in case I've lost you, let's take the same approach with exercise. Is exercise good for you? To be sure, moving and exercising your body can be very good for you, but not if you're doing it from a state of self-loathing. For example, what if a person was only exercising because they were disgusted with their body? If you approached exercise constantly thinking, "I'm fat," "I'm a slob," "I'm trash," how effective do you think exercising would be? How hard do you think it would be to actually move and exercise? It would take a lot of energy to overcome such states of negativity to move your body effectively, and it probably wouldn't be very rewarding because what you are telling your body is "I don't like you," or "I don't like me." And your body knows. Such thoughts of negativity, of lies, tell your body that it is not safe; it will not move optimally, nor will it feel amazing.

But don't take my word for it. Besides, I know this all sounds like rubbish. Let's test it. Let your body tell you whether or not what I'm saying is nonsense or true. You can test what I'm telling you the exact same way we tested the position of the tongue.

Place your feet together, straighten your knees, and say to yourself out loud or in your head, *I'm a fat slob.* Now try to touch your toes. Notice how it feels and how far you can reach. Now, say to yourself, *That's not true. I am wonderfully made. I am not a fat slob,* and try to touch your toes again. How did that feel, and how far were you able to reach? That's pretty amazing, isn't it? Your body knows the truth. Your nervous system wants to feel safe. The truth makes it feel safe. Negativity and lies make it feel unsafe.

If this is melting your brain, consider a pet. Your dog or cat knows if you love it. Your pet also knows if you are angry, scared, or sad. They genuinely know you. Likewise, your body genuinely knows you, too. It knows how you really feel, and it responds. Exercising from a state of self-loathing only fools you, it does not fool your body. And your body can't give you what you "think you should do." It can only give you what you want or what you believe because you don't actually believe in what you are doing. Instead, you are experiencing and creating your reality from the thoughts and beliefs in your subconscious. There is no amount of exercise in the world that can overcome those beliefs and give you a different outcome. The body is a great pet. It will follow or respond to what you are truly telling it from the messages you keep deep within your heart. Does this make sense?

We could take this same view with any action we partake in or any input we try to give our nervous system. We often labor in vain, attempting "good works" through exercise, diet, volunteering, etc. We labor in vain, not because these works aren't good but because our hearts are telling our nervous system a different story. We lack integrity between what we keep in our hearts and what we do. On the surface, we try to do the "right" things, but in the depths of our hearts, we aren't always telling the truth about who we are or what we believe. My point is, as we mature and grow, our experiences become determined by our subconscious beliefs and thoughts. So if we want to have an optimal life experience, one filled with health and joy, we must sow the truth in our hearts.

Notice the proverb says to "keep your heart with all diligence." This means we can protect our hearts and determine what thoughts and beliefs we allow them to have. But the only way to change these thoughts and beliefs is to uncover them and let them go by planting something else in their place.

This can be done, but it is not necessarily easy. That word *diligence* is the key. Diligence is being aware or awake to the issues we are storing in our subconscious minds. If we want to protect our hearts and ultimately determine the course of our lives, our bodies, and everything else we desire to experience, we must be diligent and intent on becoming and being our greatest selves.

Otherwise, if we sleep and allow our subconscious mind to store unsafe and untrue information, we are pretty much programming the DNA of our soul with a self-destruct sequence. We'll become a ticking time bomb that time will indeed touch.

Programming Our DNA

Again, the only way to keep our hearts is through awareness. This means we have to wake up and use our conscious minds to become aware of what's playing in the background or in the depths of our subconscious minds. We cannot afford to be "asleep at the wheel" and expect that we will end up in paradise. If we want to get to Eden, it's going to have to be with our eyes wide open.

We are creators. We are an expression of our input, of what we plant inside of our minds. We get to control or determine our expressions and experiences. We can even influence how our physical genetic code is released by the thoughts and choices we make.[3] That's right—your thoughts are that powerful. They are strong enough to affect the genetic expression of your genes. Our thoughts and actions penetrate the DNA of our cells. Just because you have undesirable genes doesn't mean they will unfold inside of you. Conversely, just because you have great genes doesn't mean you'll express them to their fullest potential either. It's the codes or the thoughts you keep in your subconscious mind, in your heart, that determines your ultimate expression.

You may have noticed that I have been weaving different words in and out above like truth and lies, safe and unsafe, and thrive and survive. I've even said some weird things like the truth makes your body feel safe, and your body knows the truth. All of this is, well, *true*.

Your body is a vessel for life—your life. It's like your jacket or your pants. You fill it, you animate it, you express yourself through it. It is not just any jacket, though. It's connected to you. It knows your thoughts. It knows your emotions. It knows the truth about you, and it even knows the truth that you do not know. If you hold the wrong thoughts, your body knows. This can be seen in how you move and feel. I know all of this sounds like a fantasy, but

---

[3] Todd Harnagan, Wellness, the 5 Essential Elements (New York: Gallup Press) p. 74.

if you are curious enough to explore what I'm saying, it could change your life forever.

Your body is a living vessel for Life and Wisdom. It can discern the difference between truth and lies. The truth is "safe," it feels good. A lie, or falsehood, is "not safe," it doesn't feel good. Your nervous system responds to the truth. I know this is a wild thought, but it's also a beautiful one as well.

The Life inside of you can guide you even when you don't consciously know the truth. If the thoughts you are keeping inside of your subconscious are lies, your body can tell you as those thoughts affect it. If the thoughts you hold in your heart are truth, your body can show you that as well. Do you remember when we tested the thought *I'm a fat slob*, versus *I am beautiful and I'm wonderfully made*? One of those statements allowed you to move better than the other. Even if you didn't believe either statement, your body expressed the truth about them.

You with me yet? It doesn't matter as much what you believe, and that does matter for sure, but what matters more is the *truth* of what you believe. Yes, your beliefs will determine your outcome, your expressions, and your reality, but what if those outcomes were based more on the truth of your beliefs than your actual beliefs? What if your expressions were the result of lies or falsehoods that you held as your beliefs? We know people "catch a cold" or get the flu when they believe they are going to do so; they've planted that belief in their heart. But what if the real reason they got the flu was because they've sown a lie into their heart? What if holding lies or falsehoods leads to negative expressions? Or, what if holding certain expectations leads to certain experiences and outcomes? People generally recover from a cold or flu after a few days to a few weeks, but the truth is, once they "catch" the virus, they typically expect to recover from it.

Yes, you could make the argument that it is a person's immune system that prevents them from getting sick or that helps them to recover from a cold at a certain rate, but the health of the immune system is a by-product of the health of an individual's nervous system, and the health of an individual's nervous system is representative of their mental and emotional health which often flows from their subconscious thoughts. Basically, the mind leads the body and determines the expressions and capabilities of all its systems.

People also age and grow frail with "itises," inflammations like arthritis, and other conditions when they <u>believe</u> they are getting old. They accept the conventional wisdom that the body breaks down as it ages. These beliefs are lies that weaken the body. Unlike recovering from a cold, the reason these aged conditions do not undo themselves is because people don't expect or believe their youth will return to them once they believe they are getting old. They keep holding onto the conventional wisdom (the lie), and they express its curse.

So as you can see, believing you are aging is far more dangerous than believing you will catch a cold or the flu. Once a person gets a general sickness, they typically believe it will pass. Once a person settles on the notion that they are aging, they resign themselves to that idea, and they do not plant the truth to replace the lie of aging that they are holding in their hearts.

Again, our outcomes are the results of our inputs, or the information we keep and continue to send to our brains. As far as your youth and vitality are concerned, your body does what you tell it to do. It listens to your deepest inner thoughts, the ones you don't even know about. It wants to be vibrant and useful, but it only rises to the level of nourishment you supply it through truth or falsehood.

The truth feels better than a lie, and your body wants to express the truth. The saying that "the truth shall set you free" could have many layers to it because the truth can set you free to move and express your true self. It can reveal the original YOU.

If it's really the truth about what you believe that matters, how can you tell if what you think is true or not? Test your range of motion or strength over an issue. If a question or statement is true, you'll move pretty well and be pretty strong. If a question or statement is false, your range of motion will diminish and so will your strength. This expression/reaction happens at the speed of your nervous system. So, ask the question. Test your body. Discover what you can learn. Truth is life and it allows you to express yourself without restriction. Falsehood is death, and it puts the brakes on your body. Death doesn't feel safe in the nervous system. Truth feels safe.

THE SPIRIT OF YOU(TH)

"I think as we get older we tend to give up on things."
- Glenn Lee

I'm not asking you to believe me. I'm inviting you to investigate this for yourself. There is inherent wisdom inside of you. It knows the difference between truth and falsehood, and it expresses that difference. *Out of your heart, the issues of life flow.* That's powerful, especially if you can learn to guard, or garden, your heart. Gardening your heart does not happen by accident. It requires you to be intentional about what you think, what you believe, what you hear, what you see, and what you consider. It requires you to seek out the truth of a matter and not blindly accept erroneous information that others try to feed you. It may also require you to let go of a great deal of information you once believed, or overhaul your entire mental framework of beliefs and knowledge.

Holding onto false information can be a lot like holding a stack of logs in your arms. If you were holding a tall stack of wood in your arms, it might obscure your ability to see and cause you to stumble as you walk. It would also take a great deal of energy to continue to hold all that wood if you never put it down. BUT, If you let the tall stack of wood go, you could see clearly where to put your feet, and you could put your energy into easily stepping and walking to your destination. Likewise, the truth is always there to be seen, and it requires much less energy than holding onto false information.

If you are still with me, if you tested your range of motion or strength by asking questions or making statements and you found changes, perhaps thought interrupting changes, I have some more questions for you:

Who are you asking?

What are you asking to determine the truth?

Are you asking your body to tell you the truth?

Or are you using your body to demonstrate and express the truth?

If you were to ask the question, "Am I wonderfully made?" and you discovered your range of motion to be improved, indicating a "YES, I am wonderfully made" answer, who did you ask? What gave you the answer?

Let's explore this a little further. I am going to ask you to keep an open mind. An open mind, a genuine quest to know the truth, is essential when asking questions. Asking a question to prove you are right or to leverage a situation is not asking a question in sincere openness. Also, asking a question in disgust or disbelief, or asking a question thinking you already know the answer is not asking a question with a genuine desire for truth. If you want to know the truth, you need to lay down your defenses, your beliefs, your judgments, and your opinions—you need to be a blank canvas ready for pure creation. Be open. That's my ask of you.

I'm going to share another quote with you. You can even test what I'm about to share with you for yourself, to discover whether or not it is true. But consider this quote from the Bible (again, please keep an open mind):

> *"Or do you not know that your body is the temple of the Holy Spirit who is in you, whom you have from God, and you are not your own?"* - 1 Corinthians 6:19, NKJV

Please don't let religion close your mind. And please feel free to replace the words "Holy Spirit" with Creation, with the Universe, with God, with Energy, with Wisdom, with I Am, with Light, with Life, or the Source. But what if Creation Itself, the One who designed you, could speak through your body to help you determine truth from falsehood? What if eternal youth and vitality (power) could strengthen your body throughout every moment in every season of your life? What if your body wasn't really you, but the expression of the life you hold inside of you? Have you tested this question yet: "Is my body the temple of the Creator?" What did your body tell you? Did you move better or worse?

If you moved better, what do you think that means? If you moved worse, let me ask you some follow-up questions: Did you ask the question in fear? Did you ask the question in disbelief or disgust? Were you open?

If we genuinely seek the truth through curiosity, the Wisdom will guide us. If we are asking for truth through a veil of negativity, are we really seeking the truth? Darkness runs from the Light, not toward it. If none of this makes any sense to you whatsoever, I'd like to introduce you to a few concepts that may help.

The 15 Commitments of Conscious Power

In the past few years, I have come across two books that have had a profound impact on my life: *The 15 Commitments of Conscious Leadership*[4] by Jim Dethmer, Diana Chapman, Kaley Warner Klemp, and *Power Versus Force*[5] by Dr. David Hawkins. The concepts in these books were life-changing for me: I cannot recommend them enough. The books are completely unrelated, but in my mind, they can be perfectly woven together to help you realize the life and the strength you were designed to have. I am going to attempt to weave them together for you here.

I Walk the Line

> *"I keep a close watch on this heart of mine. I keep my eyes wide open all the time."* - Johnny Cash, *I Walk the Line*

The 15 Commitments of Conscious Leadership is written to elevate the consciousness of leaders, which means this book is for everyone. We are all leaders, whether we know it or not. Anyway, to me, the most brilliant idea in the whole book is the idea that there is a line of consciousness. As a leader, you are either operating below the line of consciousness or above the line of consciousness.

If you are operating below the line, you are being a "To me" leader or a "By me" leader. A "To me" leader would be someone who believes things happen to them. A "By me" leader would be someone who believes things happen because of them. Both a "To me" and a "By me" leader

---

[4] Jim Dethmer, Diana Chapman, & Kaley Klemp, The 15 Commitments to Conscious Leadership (Chapman and Klemp, 2014)
[5] Dr. David R. Hawkins, Power Versus Force (Hay House: 2002)

operate from the ego, or the self. They are "me" oriented. This type of leadership is limited in what it can accomplish, and it carries a great deal of energy cost with it as it is often fear-driven, meaning it takes a great deal of energy to maintain. Below-the-line leaders are those who let their emotions control them. They don't listen to the needs of others. They would rather "win" a discussion or debate than achieve the greatest possible outcome for their team, their company, or their mission. Basically, a below-the-line leader is constantly telling their nervous system, "It's not safe." They are always on guard, ready to fight or defend their position. In a neurological sense, a below-the-line leader lives in the sympathetic state, the "fight-or-flight" state or the "survival" state.

If you are operating above the line, you are said to be a "Through me" leader or an "As me" leader. A "Through me" leader is a leader who knows things unfold through him, not because of him. An "As me" leader is a leader who knows Creation is living and expressing Itself as the leader. Both of these leadership styles are beautiful. They are driven toward the greatest good for all the people involved, and they seek the best outcomes. This type of leadership is effortless; it is flow, meaning these leaders are simply the willing vessels of the greatest good. They see others, they control their emotions, they control their thoughts, and they allow something greater than themselves to operate in their place. Above-the-line leaders are constantly telling their nervous system, "It is safe." Neurologically speaking, above-the-line leaders operate from the parasympathetic state, the "rest and digest" state, or the "thrive" state.

The easiest way to explain the leadership styles above and below the line is that above-the-line leaders are conscious of who they are and to what their purpose is, and below-the-line leaders are unconscious and *"they know not what they do."*[6]

---

[6] Luke 23:34, King James Version

All leaders can rise above and fall below the line at any time. The beautiful thing about the idea of the line is that it helps you remain conscious, and it allows you to become or operate as the type of leader (person or being) you want to be. In any situation, in any conversation, in any action, the line invites you to ask this simple question: "Am I above the line or below the line?" This question is sobering. It causes you to pause and check where you are. If you are below the line, it allows you to make a shift and rise above it. It allows you the chance to make a conscious switch in your autonomic nervous system and take it from the "fight-or-flight" mode to the "rest-and-digest" mode.

Why am I telling you about this?

Because being awake to who you are and where you are operating from can help you make a shift toward where you want to be. You can't optimize your potential and live a life of vitality if you are asleep at the wheel or if you are driven by unconscious fears. But if you become aware that fear is gripping you, that anger is spurring you, or that a grudge is what's nudging you, you can consciously make a shift to let those weights go and rise above the line. This is important because in the search for the original you, being below the line consumes a great amount of energy. It takes a great deal of energy to hold onto negativity: to fears, to resentment, to anger, to unforgiveness, to offenses. It takes a great deal of effort to defend your position or attack the opposition.

The original you had a ton of endless and boundless energy because you weren't using it to hold onto negativity and all the energy-consuming thoughts and muscle tension that comes with holding negativity. This negativity will both shorten and rob the quality of your life. It ages you because it consumes you.

But living above the line is effortless. This is how you started out in the world as a child, above the line. This is where life is found. Boundless joy and endless energy are above the line, and this is where they flow from you and as you.

Real life and real power are found above the line, and so is the real you.

The Power of Truth

The other book I mentioned, *Power Versus Force,* is one of the most fascinating books I've ever read. One of the major concepts of this book is that Power comes from Truth; it is effortless and gentle. And Force comes from Falsehood; it is burdensome and violent. We are meant to operate from Power and not from Force. Another major concept in this book is that we can discern the difference between truth and falsehood through biofeedback testing (testing the body as we did earlier in the book).

Through extensive research, Dr. Hawkins even established a calibrated scale of consciousness; I like to think of it as a "spectrum of truth" scale. It's a logarithmic scale that offers a value to the level of truth on any given thing. The scale ranges from 0 to 1,000. In Dr. Hawkins's scale, truth begins at courage, which he has calibrated at 200. Anything below 200 is a falsehood. For your understanding, here are some things that are scored below 200: fear, anger, bitterness, jealousy, depression, apathy (all "negative" states). Here are things that Dr. Hawkins calibrated above 200: acceptance, intelligence, love, compassion, joy, and bliss.

If we are operating from falsehood, below courage at 200 on Dr. Hawkins's scale, then we are not going to be living our best life. It's very much the same as being a "below-the-line leader." Operating below 200, operating from fear and all of its cousins, takes energy. It keeps us in fight or flight and ultimately burns us out. None of us were made to be afraid. None of us were made to live a life of fear. A life lived in fear robs us of our vitality and darkens our experiences. It keeps us on the run, on the edge, and on the defense. If we cannot rise to courage, to the level of truth, we cannot thrive. Instead, we scrap and fight to survive. This isn't a life; it's a hell. None of us were meant for hell.

"This is the Way" - The Mandalorian Creed

As I said, these two books became one in my mind. I have combined their concepts to help me stay awake and be aware of who I am and where I want to be. Ultimately, I want to optimize the expression and the experience of who I am; I'm seeking to live the abundant life, as we all should. We were all designed to live a life of vitality, to live a life of boundless joy and energy, the life we see all children demonstrate.

Just like the Three Pillars of Human Movement come together to establish our default movement patterns, our default way of being (our original selves) is to operate and function from the states of joy and wonder. This is more than evident in the facial expressions of any developing child. It is as if beams of pure light flow from their eyes. This is the way it is meant to be. That's the foundation of life we were all meant to live from. Beneath all the structures we learn from the world, beneath the thoughts, the language, the rules, and the circumstances we collect, there is a foundation of pure joy. We never lose this foundation because we can never lose our original self. It's like our inheritance; it's just ours to have. We can return to our default way of being. We can rediscover our original self.

How can we return to this default way of being? How can we restore our foundation of joy and wonder? I think this is where the awareness comes in. Well, awareness and desire. We have to want to return to this state of being. We have to want "more" out of this life, and we have to maintain awareness of who we really are and *where* we are.

This is where the line comes in. If we can maintain an awareness of where we are in relationship to "the line," we can make intentional shifts to either let go of negative issues or thoughts, or we can reach for positive states above the line. Basically, if we become aware of ourselves, we can make the necessary shifts we need to make in order to return to our original states of joy and bliss.

"The Kingdom of Heaven is within you." You've likely heard that phrase before. In relationship to the line, if we are above the line, we are living in the kingdom. If we are below the line, we are living in hell. So we have a choice. We can be unconscious and live in hell, or we can be alert and choose to live in heaven.

This is where being conscious gives us power. It's also where I'm going to try to connect the dots between *The 15 Commitments of Conscious Leadership* and *Power vs. Force*!

Power = Truth = Love = Safe = Joy = Peace = Thrive = Vitality = Life = YOU(th)

---------- Courage ---- 200 ---- Willingness ----------

Force = Falsehood = Fear = Unsafe = Defeat = Defend / Fight = Survive = Weary = Death

According to Dr. Hawkins, Truth starts at courage, 200 on his scale of consciousness. I'm saying Courage is "the Line," as referenced in *The 15 Commitments to Conscious Leadership*. I'm also going to redefine courage and add willingness to its meaning. Being courageous is also being willing—willing to let go, or willing to reach higher. Either way, courage requires willingness.

Being aware of the line, being aware of where we are in relationship to the line, allows us to make a cognitive change. If we are below the line, we are suffering in our own hell. If we are above the line, we are discovering the kingdom of heaven. The deeper we are below the line, the more we suffer and the less vitality we have. The higher we are above the line, the closer we are to our original state of being in joy, wonder, and bliss, and the more life we experience.

As I hoped to illustrate earlier, you can test this out for yourself. You can determine if any of this is true by how your body responds to your thoughts, your questions, and your emotions. If you are living above the line, you are operating in Truth, and your nervous system will feel safe. You will move and feel better. You will have life flowing from you; fountains of living water will be flowing out of you, and you will nourish others with your life. This is much the same as when the light of a newborn child fills the room and floods into the hearts of all those around him.

If you are living below the line, you are operating in Falsehood and illusion, and your nervous system will not feel safe. You will be in the all-too-consuming survival mode (fight or flight). You will be anxious, tense, afraid, irritable, and you will feel like "blah." Life won't be flowing from you, but negativity will, and it will try to infect those around you. This is much the same as when the darkness of a person drains the energy or agitates the energy of an entire room.

The point is, we are meant to live above the line in paradise. I know this because this is the state we all entered the world in; when we arrived here, we were above the line. This is where life is full of abundant energy, strength, and vitality. This is where the original you is found, where you discover your true self. We can only live above the line through vigilant conscious choice and desire. To live above the line is to choose to protect our hearts so that our natural default way of being (our foundation of joy and wonder) flows from us.

But if we sleep, if we are not aware of who we are and what we do, if we don't keep watch over our hearts, we will sink below the line, and life will be drained from us. It takes massive amounts of energy to live life below the line.

I'll be honest. I've been beating around the bush, so here is what I really want to say. To live above the line, to live "As Me" or "Through Me," is to be One with Creation and experience its life flow to you and from you. To live below the line, to live "To me," or "By me," is to be ruled by your ego and separated from Creation; not that Creation will separate from you, but that you are asleep to the Life that is in you.

In the hope that I can explain what I'm trying to say clearly, I've made the following chart:

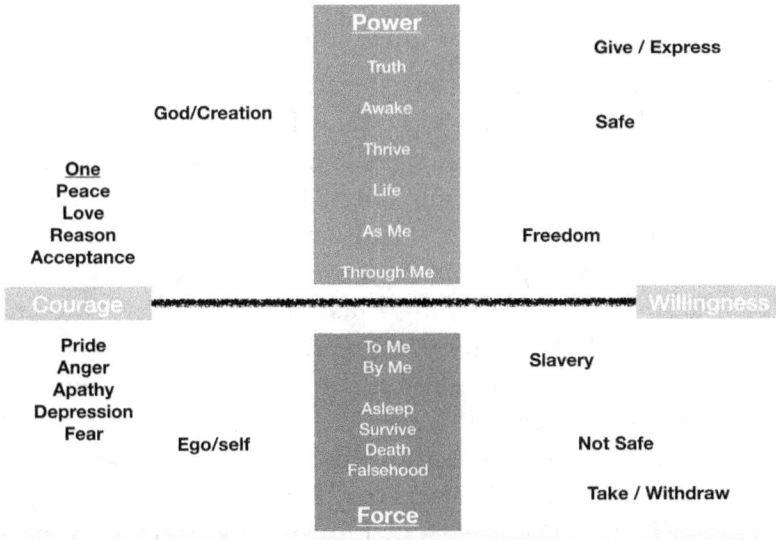

Looking at my chart above, living above the line is to live in our true default state of being. This was our original foundational state when we were children. You may not remember it, but I'm sure you can recognize it in other children.

Living below the line is our corrupted state. This is the state we learned, accumulated, and adopted as we grew. This is the state often experienced through our mental framework of how the world works. It was crafted by our ego through the knowledge we have been collecting from birth.

It is fear-based and fear-driven, geared toward survival—the survival of our ego.

Don't get me wrong; fear is and can be valuable when it comes to the physical survival of the body. But in today's modern world, if we find ourselves below the line, it probably has very little to do with the survival of our body and more to do with the survival of our ego.

To live above the line is to live in freedom as your original self. It leads to being One with Creation. It is powerful, it is lovely, it is safe, it is effortless, and it radiates Life.

To be below the line is bondage. It is a life of fear forced onto the world by the ego's lies and scare tactics. It divides and separates everything for personal gain but ultimately destroys the very life it pretends to save.

If what I'm trying to explain is still unclear, I get it. This is so deep I am finding I just don't have the words to do it justice. I am in good company, though. Throughout all of time, others have also tried to explain this same, rich concept. Just in case it helps, I'll share two passages of Scripture that may explain what I'm trying to say better than I can. Please understand that I am only using the Bible because I am familiar with it. This same Wisdom is found in other texts from other disciplines. It is just worded a bit differently.

THE SPIRIT OF YOU(TH)

"This is my command—be strong and courageous! Do not be afraid or discouraged. For the Lord your God is with you wherever you go." - Joshua 1:9, New Living Translation

This passage is saying that we should live our lives above the line. That is where Creation intends us to be. We are not to be afraid. We are not to be sad, depressed, or discouraged. We are not to be angry or bitter. We are to be willing to rest in God. That is where courage starts.

Those who are One with God shall become like Him. They shall be strengthened and rise up on wings like eagles. They will run and never grow weary, they will walk and never faint. - Isaiah 40:31 (I paraphrased it)

This passage is saying that when we realize we are one with Creation, Creation will flow from us as us. It will be the life that pours out of us, much like the boundless life and energy that flows from joyful, playful children. We won't grow weary. We won't grow weak. We will continually rise up and soar with the strength of an eagle. Remember, eagles only know how to fly. They do not retire their wings when they grow old. They don't even know they are old. This is the way for us as well.

Again, I ask that you don't believe what I'm saying. To believe me just gives away your power. I am inviting you to investigate this and consider if what I'm sharing is true or not. Study this chapter, look over my diagram. But test for yourself if what I'm saying is true. Ask questions, let Life answer you. Let the answers you discover become your input so they can affect your output. YOU must experience this to know if any of it is true or not. Don't blindly accept it; that is being asleep. Test it; that's being awake.

Remember, it's all about input. What we feed our bodies determines our expressions. The body follows and expresses what is in the heart, the thoughts and beliefs we keep buried there. The line and all of its implications stem from our hearts. Fear, anger, joy, bliss, sadness, truth, and lies are all sown in our hearts. Our bodies and our lives bear the fruit of what we sow.

To sum this entire chapter up, the heart is the fertile ground that determines our experiences. Whatever we sow, we reap.

ARE WE WHAT WE EAT?

Given all that I just shared about our thoughts and beliefs, there is still one more input or source of information I want to talk about: food. Nutrition is an input, and it does matter as it influences our expressions. We all know this. It is fairly simple to understand, and yet we've made it the most complicated subject known to man.

I could write over 1,000 pages on the subject of nutrition. I could regurgitate studies on eating meat, on eating only plants, I could talk about macro and micronutrients, essential fats, inflammatory foods, fiber, and anything else we've "learned" over the last 100 years about food. And if I were to fill 1,000 pages with nothing but facts about food and nutrition, I would only be drawing a line in the sand and all that would be interpreted would ultimately be "Us versus Them," or "Good versus Bad," or "Right versus Wrong."

Which brings me to my point about food. It's not just about what we eat (and yes, it really does matter—some), it's also about *how* we eat, from the actual mechanical process of eating to the labels that we place on food, and the beliefs we have about food. As I tried to illustrate earlier with my chocolate chip cookie example, our beliefs about food could trump the actual food we eat.

This means *how* we eat could be more important than *what* we eat. Before we go further, please understand I'm not saying nutrients and food sources don't matter. They absolutely do. But really they don't—if we can't get nutrients out of the food we eat because we are not going about eating in the best way.

Your thoughts can prevent you from digesting your food and absorbing its nutrients. Your beliefs, whether gained from Dr. Oz, or your parents, or your religion will greatly determine what "good" the food you consume can do. Your thoughts and beliefs could even flip healthy food upside down to where it is actually not "good" for you. We've discussed this already. If our body is trying to survive due to fears, beliefs, false thinking, and lies, it isn't going to optimally make great use of the nutrients it receives from food. It will not be concerned with resting and digesting, but more concerned with fighting and flighting.

We tend to rigidly hold onto ideals when it comes to food. For example, the source and type of food does matter, yes. But that knowledge, being rigidly held, can also be a thought trap in itself. If you believe organic is the only way to go, and all other non-organic food is toxic, what will happen to you if you can't buy organic food? What will happen to your body if you have to eat non-organic food, believing it is toxic? Do you think this will cause a stress response in your emotions and your body?

My point is that we can't always control where our food comes from. Most of us are only blindly believing the labels on the food in the first place. Surely marketers wouldn't lie to us, right? Anyway, if we can't always control where our food is sourced, there may be times when we just have to eat what is available, or we just have to eat in order to live. In those times, and in all times, it would be best to approach eating more from a *how* perspective because even in tough situations, the one thing we can control is how we eat and how we approach a meal.

So really, it is how we eat, how we approach food that may matter the most. We can approach how we eat in two ways—this is the same approach we will be using to restore and rediscover our you(th), by the way:

1) We will look at our physical design and engage it appropriately.
2) We will work to approach our meals from above the line.

The Miracle of Eating

> *"Blessed is the lion that the human will eat, so that the lion becomes human."* - The Gospel of Thomas, *The Nag Hammadi Scriptures*

Have you ever considered the miraculous events that take place when you eat? To be honest, this is something I've just come to realize, but our bodies are literally what we eat. We've all heard that before, and we all know it, but I'm guessing we think of it this way: "healthy food" makes us "healthy" and "junk food" makes us feel "junky." But the miracle of nutrition is much deeper than that because whatever we eat actually becomes us. When we eat food, our body performs a miracle and transforms that food into *us*, building our bones, muscles, cells, neurons, and thoughts.

In Yoga, our body is called the *food body* because it is a collection of the food we have gathered and used to build ourselves. When you think about how we are designed, how we eat and become, it's really quite amazing.

So it is no surprise that our body is designed to take in food, break it down into usable components, and then replenish, build, and energize itself. This process happens best in the parasympathetic mode of our autonomic nervous system—the rest-and-digest mode. Digestion is the process of breaking down our food into usable components or nutrients. Absorption is the process of actually being able to absorb the nutrients so they can be sent where they need to go. For the sake of simplicity, let's just say absorption is part of the digestion process. Digestion happens optimally when the nervous system feels safe. If the nervous system does not feel safe, digestion is not a priority.

Digestion also best happens when the design of the body and its digestive system is fully engaged in. For example, we have certain structures, like teeth, intended to perform certain functions, like chew, to enable us to optimally digest our food. Not chewing our food would be like sabotaging the process of digestion. If the stomach is expecting pulverized mush to digest and instead it gets hunks and chunks of uncrushed food, the other parts of the digestive system may have to work harder and may not function optimally. It's much the same as how the body moves. If the ankle is not fully mobile, the knee and hip have to work harder and less efficiently than they are intended to. A non-moving part creates a chain of events that can result in pain and injury. Likewise, a skipped step in the digestion process can also create a chain of events that can lead to other issues, including pain and inflammation.

Therefore, it stands to reason that how we go about eating food determines how well we can digest our food. How well we digest food is a determinant of the outcome of our health. I'm about to share two super-simple but powerful things you can do physically to help you get the biggest digestion bang for your buck:

1) Pause and breathe before you begin eating. Your breath is the "toggle switch" between the fight-or-flight mode and the rest-and-digest mode. We want to optimally digest our food, so we need to be telling our nervous system it is safe to eat. Breathing down into our belly puts the body in rest-and-digest mode.

   Before you eat, check to see where you are breathing and then take some deliberate breaths down into your belly. And, while you eat, take conscious pauses to check if you are still breathing down into your belly. This simple act can keep your body in thrive mode and allow you to more optimally digest your food. It can also help keep any negative thoughts that would send you into fight or flight at bay.

2) Chew your food. Chew it well beyond what you think is adequate. Make it a liquid before you swallow. You have molars for grinding, and your saliva has digestive enzymes in it to begin the breakdown of food (carbohydrates) in your mouth. Incidentally, if your saliva has enzymes to break down carbohydrates, it would appear that the body is made and intended to ingest carbohydrates. I know you know this, I'm just pointing it out to highlight the design.

   Anyway, if you pulverize and liquidize your food as best you can—no matter if it is meat, carbs, or fat—it will be easier for your stomach and intestines to further break down the food, and you will get more nutrients out of the food using less energy. You will also not be wasting food that you eat by passing food pieces that were too large to digest. If you chew your food well, you may find that you can eat less and feel better. You may also find that it takes you longer to eat, giving your body time to tell you when it has had enough food.

Another benefit of liquifying your food before you swallow is that you will find more enjoyment in eating. It is satisfying. It also gives you more time to listen and enjoy the company of others while you eat. A satisfying meal with great company and conversation is where the best memories in life are made.

There are two more things you can do to optimize your digestion and keep your body in Thrive mode. These two things aren't physical, and they require more of a mental presence. However, if you can implement these two things, you'll eat much better and you'll strengthen your health.

1) Don't judge. Don't judge your food, and don't judge yourself. The moment you label your food as good or bad, you are setting yourself up for nutritional hell. And the moment you pass judgment on yourself for what you have eaten, you have destined yourself to a life of slavery. As we've discussed earlier, these judgments get planted into your heart. These are the thoughts and beliefs that the issues of life spring from. If we have critical thoughts, we are condemned.

Okay, this may be one of the hardest things for you to do, but the reward is priceless…let go. Let go of your thoughts about food—the scientific thoughts, the religious thoughts, the talk-show thoughts, the Google thoughts. *All* the thoughts. Don't judge your food. Be open to it. Allow your body to decide what to make of it. I know this sounds crazy, but your body knows way more about food and what to make of it than your mind does.

You also need to learn how to let go of the judging thoughts you hold about yourself. You are not fat. You are not lazy. You're not a slob. You're not ugly. You're not old. Don't hold those thoughts in your heart; they only direct your body where to go. They tell your body what to do with the food that you eat! Let those thoughts go. Instead, learn to focus on the truth: You're strong. You're perfect. You're just right. Let your body know that. You'd be surprised at what it can do.

2) Be grateful. When you eat, approach each meal with gratitude. Real, joyful gratitude, not ritual gratitude. Genuine gratitude for receiving a meal, regardless of what it is, blesses the meal you are eating. It is a declaration of joyful thankfulness that soothes your nervous system and allows your body to freely and efficiently make use of the meal.

Ritual gratitude is not genuine. It's a ritual and most often unconsciously laced with your true feelings and thoughts. When you approach a meal with gratitude, you are approaching that meal from above the line. You are allowing your body the opportunity to digest that food and transform it into vitality and vigor.

Truthfully, you could also approach every situation in your life the same way, with gratitude. This doesn't have to only be applied to meals, but meals are an easy place to start practicing. Test this out for yourself and try it for one week. At each meal, be present enough to be genuinely grateful for your meal and your body. See if this does not make a difference in how you feel.

Do this when you eat:

Breathe deep into your belly. Then, in your head or your heart, out loud or in silence, bless your food with gratitude. Don't label it, and don't label yourself. Just be thankful. Then, take a bite of your food and put your utensil down, or put the food down. While still breathing through your nose, down into your belly, chew your food until it is basically like a liquid, and then swallow it. Then pick up your utensil or food and repeat this process again and again until you are done with your meal. While you are eating, it is completely okay to continue to be grateful and joyful as you experience your meal.

You're welcome.

If you learn how to eat this way, it can really change your life.

The point is, while it does matter what you eat, it matters more *how* you eat. An open mind, a little gratitude, and a restful heart can help you get more nutrients out of a chocolate chip cookie than what a self-condemning mind will allow your body to squeeze out of a leaf of kale. When you eat, eat above the line.

THE KINGDOM OF YOU(TH)

"When you stop learning, you die." - Danny Dillon

My father-in-law, Danny Dillon, said that a few years ago. He is in his seventies, but he has the mental and physical agility of a young man, and most men half his age. We were talking about personal strengths, desires, and personalities (what makes people who they are) when he said, "When you stop learning, you die." When he said that, it was as if a mental bomb went off in my head. At the time, there were no thoughts in my head to dissect what he said, but the statement left a crater big enough to stay with me. I've never forgotten it. And now, I'm getting it.

There is an art to maintaining our youth, and I think it is found in the continuation of *being*. Learning—true learning—is the unfolding of you(th). Learning is not just accepting what you are told, and it's certainly not just collecting facts. Learning is not just academic. It's not just about math, science, and language. Learning is also discovering. It's curiosity being quenched. It's a realization of truth.

When we stop learning things, when we stop discovering, when we are no longer curious, and when we stop realizing who we are, then we die. We may not die a physical death at that point, but that is the point when we stop unfolding and becoming. It is the point where we stop being and enjoying our true selves. When we no longer seek to learn and grow, we shrink, wither, and die. We give in to lies, and we let go of life.

Life is youth, a constant revealing of energy and strength. It is ageless. Seek if this is true. Either ask the question and test it as you now know how or simply experience it for yourself.

If you want to experience it right now, close your eyes. Well, after you read this, close your eyes. But close your eyes and place your attention inside yourself. Don't move or think, just feel. Feel your breath, feel the energy in your body, in your hands, in your head, in your heart. Is that energy old? Is it tired? Can it age? What gives life to your imagination? To your daydreams? To your thoughts? If you just sit there and feel, can you not feel youth? It's not until you try to move, or look in the mirror, or ache that you feel and believe in an alternative. But the life in you does not age; it is forever young. You may not experience it in your day-to-day life, but you can at any time if you seek it and engage in it.

When we settle for lies and alternatives, we stop seeking, learning, discovering, and growing. We replace living with knowing. This is existence; it's not life, but death. This is where we set aside our youth because we are not using it.

Again, the energetic joy and light that was in you as a small child is still in you right now. It is your default state of being, the ageless energy and power that is in you. As a child, that ageless energy delighted in using you. As an adult, you must delight in using it.

Youth reveals what we can do when we are young, but youth asks what we want to do when we are older. If we want to do nothing, it allows us to. If we want to soar through life on the wings of eagles, it will lift us up. But it only does what we ask of it based on how we engage it, whether we are settled or whether we are in this life for the long adventure. Remember, if we use it, we will have it. If we don't use it, we will lose it (or misplace it).

So if you want to live a life of youth, strength, health, and vitality, then you have to ask for it. How do you ask for it? That's the simple part. You engage in it through the physical design of your body and the intentional, mindful guarding of your heart, thoughts, and intentions. In other words, you use your body as it was designed, and you maintain awareness of who you were created to be and who you want to be. This is how you invite youth to dance with you throughout your life—you use it.

Youth soothes your nervous system and tells it that it is safe. Youth knows no fear; it's courageous. Youth approaches life from above the line. It is the limitless energy of a child and the joy of a thrilling adventure. Through the eyes of youth, everything is brand new in every moment, just like you are. And through the heart of youth, everything is a giggle and a smile. What I mean is that when you are dancing in your youth, you don't smile—*you* are the smile, and joy gushes from you like a fountain of living water.

So, if you're still here, still seeking your youth, it's in you. You just need to remember how to delight in using it again. So let's learn to do that.

A DAILY MOVEMENT ROUTINE

I think the easiest way to rediscover our youth is to start with movement, again. We used movement to build ourselves up when we came into the world, and we can return to movement again to begin restoring our youth. When we were young, our design guided us through certain movements to knit our bodies together. Now we are going to return to that design and honor the Three Pillars of Human Movement in order to restore our youth. As we do this, we are also going to honor the design of our structure and attempt to nourish all of our joints, muscles, tendons, fascia, and sensory nerves.

Essentially, we are going to ask our youth if it would care to dance with us once again, and we are going to do this by moving in all the ways we were made to move. If you want something from your body, you have to make your intentions known. If you ask of it, if you challenge it through use, it will grant you what you want through adaptation. Create the demand, and your nervous system will create the supply.

We are going to approach this much the same way you did as a child, daily. As a child, you showed up every day to move and grow. That's the hardest thing we need to do now, simply show up to move and become. Every day, we are going to go through a series of movements that honor our full movement design. For each movement, we are going to perform 21 repetitions.

Why 21 repetitions? Well, I've been told 21 is considered to be a perfect number. Who am I to mess with perfection? AND, it seems to me, especially in the United States, that the age of 21 is the turning point—or the letting go point—of our youth. Here, in the US, 21 is about the age where we say, "Now what?" Maybe we graduate, maybe we look for a job in the real unsheltered world, maybe we quit being active, maybe we begin drinking and being an "adult," or whatever. But, in my mind, the early twenties is the last rally of our youth before we decide to let it go. So why not reclaim it by declaring 21 repetitions of movement as a symbol for not letting go of 21 but holding on to it? If that doesn't resonate with you, 21 daily repetitions of anything adds up to 7,665 repetitions of each movement in a year. A nervous system that logs those numbers in a year is a strong and powerful nervous system.

So here it is, a movement approach to restoring our youth, vitality, and strength. I'm actually going to give you two 21 plans, though they can both be seen as one plan. I do them both, but I know time will be an issue for some. In the beginning, these movement routines could take 20 to 30 minutes to complete, depending on your fitness level and your desire to explore the movements. Remember, we start where we are, and we grow from there. As you grow younger, you will be able to complete each plan in around ten minutes, with a combined time of around twenty minutes. But don't focus on the time it takes to perform these routines, and please don't set your sights on time as a standard of achievement. Instead, focus on the movements and the discoveries they will bring. Focus on the youth, energy, and ability you are uncovering.

It is often hard to learn movement from reading about it and seeing movement can be the best teacher of movement. The written descriptions for the Daily 21s follow below, but here is a video resource for you to see how they are actually performed: https://www.timmyanderson.net/bonus

Okay, if you are ready to start restoring your youth, this is a great way to approach longevity and vitality from a movement design perspective.

The Daily 21s for Vitality

The following movements combine to make a daily 10- to 20-minute movement routine, depending on your level of ability and explorative nature. When you get started, if it takes you much longer than this, don't panic. Remember, you are learning, and it is okay and good to spend a little extra time learning.

These movements can be done as a "To-Do" list where you simply do them and check them off, or they can be done as an adventure in self-exploration where you attend to what your body is doing, and you learn from it. There is no right or wrong to either method; there is value in both. When completed daily, these movements will help you discover your vitality and youth, as well as your true self. (As a resource, I will provide a video demonstration of these movements.)

The Lion's Yawn

Why?
- Yawning like a lion prepares the body for movement.
- This movement lengthens and awakens the muscles.
- The Lion's Yawn can refresh the eyes, allowing them to see more clearly.
- The Lion's Yawn helps to relax and remove stress from the jaws.
    - The nerves in the face, the trigeminal nerves, are connected to the diaphragm. A big Lion's Yawn can improve the function of the diaphragm (it can help you breathe better).
- The Lion's Yawn stretches the tongue, which is connected to both the vestibular system and the diaphragm. This, too, can greatly enhance the body and prepare it for movement.

How?

We are going to approach this two ways:
- The Standing Lion's Yawn
    - Stand with your feet slightly wider than shoulder-width apart and reach your arms spread wide overhead (make a big X with your body).
    - Take a big breath in through your nose, down into your belly, and make a huge yawn releasing the air out through your throat.
        - Imagine you are a lion (or imagine what a lion looks like) and make a huge yawn while you lengthen your body from your feet to your hands.
        - As you yawn, lengthen and curl your tongue as a lion would.
    - When you have ended the yawn, relax your body.

Then, perform the
- Reaching Lion's Yawn
    - Stand with your feet slightly wider than shoulder-width apart and fold at your hips, reaching your arms out horizontally.
        - This can also be done with the hands on the ground, just the same way a lion would do it.
    - Take a big breath in through your nose, down into your belly, and make a huge yawn releasing the air out through your throat.
        - Imagine you are a lion (or imagine what a lion looks like) and make a huge yawn while you lengthen your body from your feet through your hands (again, this time your body is mimicking a lion).
        - As you yawn, lengthen and curl your tongue as a lion would.
    - When you have ended the yawn, relax your body.

Okay, we are only going to make two yawns here. For everything else, we are going to accumulate 21 repetitions of each movement. The yawns are movement preparation, and they are too amazing not to do.

Exaggerated Cross-Crawls

Why?
- Cross-crawls connect both hemispheres of the brain and strengthen the communication in the brain and throughout the nervous system.
- Exaggerated cross-crawls teach rhythm, coordination, and balance.
- Exaggerated cross-crawls connect the torso by solidifying the contra-lateral bond between the shoulders and hips.
- This movement provides gentle rotation to the spine.
- Cross-crawls help with focus, memory, and creativity.
- The exaggerated movement sends more information to the brain about where the body is and what all of its parts are doing.

How?
- Stand with feet shoulder-width apart.
- Close your lips, place your tongue on the roof of your mouth, and breathe through your nose.
    - Maintain this way of breathing throughout this movement.
- Make big, exaggerated circle-like movements with your arms as you move them to touch opposite forearms to opposite thighs.
    - This is like making huge, alternating shoulder circles while you touch opposite limbs together.
- Try to stay erect (don't bend over) while you are touching your opposing limbs together.
- Make sure you touch opposing limbs together.
    - Touch provides more information than crossing midline alone.

- Perform 21 total touches.

Infinity Circles

Why?
- Visualizing the infinity symbol, the "X" in its center uses and connects both hemispheres of the brain.
- Tracing the infinity symbol with the eyes and arms crosses the midline of the body and requires both hemispheres of the brain to work together.
- Tracing the infinity symbol with the eyes and the head activates the vestibular system, strengthening it, and it improves balance.
- This movement provides rotation, lateral flexion, and lateral extension to the spine in gentle, small ranges of motion.
- This movement takes coordinates of the visual and vestibular system and floods the nervous system with nourishing information.

How?
- Stand with feet shoulder-width apart.
- Close your lips, place your tongue on the roof of your mouth, and breathe through your nose.
  - Maintain this way of breathing throughout this movement.
- With your arms stretched out in front of your body, place your hands together as if to make the "prayer" emoji.
- Keep your eyes focused on the tips of your fingers and begin tracing the infinity symbol out in front of your body.
  - Let your head move, tilt, and rotate with the symbol, following the eyes.
  - Let your spine, hips, and legs also follow the flow and rotation of the infinity symbol as you trace it.
- Every time you cross the center of the infinity symbol, that is a repetition. Cross the center of the infinity symbol 21 times.
- Switch directions and trace the infinity in the opposite direction you just did for another 21 mid-line crossing repetitions.

Baby's Breath

Why?
- Breathing deep into the belly and letting go of tension tells the nervous system the body is safe.
- Deep belly breathing stabilizes the spine and allows for power and strength expression.
- Breathing is the "switch" between "fight or flight" and "rest and digest."
  - This can reduce, if not eliminate, stress.
- Breathing is a ladder that can help the soul approach thoughts and emotions from "above the line."
- Belly breathing through the nasal passages is truly the "Breath of Life." Willingness and Courage are found here. Acceptance and Love thrive here.
- Belly breathing can be a conscious, physical action that helps to melt away negative thoughts, emotions, the physical symptoms they create, and the reality they would make of your life.
- Breath creates the opportunity for truth to help protect the heart.

How?
- Get on your forearms and knees, sitting back over your feet.
- Rest your head wherever it is comfortable.
- Close your lips, place your tongue on the roof of your mouth, and breathe through your nose as deeply as you can.
  - Try to expand your pelvis with your breath.
- Pull air into your lungs until it wants to stop coming in. Then let it out until it decides to stop escaping.

- With each exhalation, try to let your body melt into the floor (let go of any tension you find).
- Perform 21 deep, intentional, relaxed breaths.

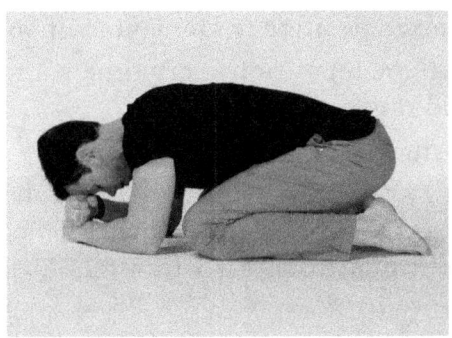

Head Nods

Why?
- Head Nods activate the vestibular system and strengthen its connection to the muscles of the torso.
- Head Nods coordinate the visual and vestibular system, solidifying their connection.
- Head Nods move the cervical spine through flexion and extension.

How?
- From the Baby's Breath position, close your lips, place your tongue on the roof of your mouth, and breathe through your nose.
  o Maintain this way of breathing throughout this movement
- Using your eyes, look up and lift your head to where it will comfortably go.

- Then, using your eyes, look down and lower your head to where it will comfortably go.
  - Don't allow your head to drop and flop. Control it.
  - As you lower your head, move through a chin-tucked position (move your chin to your throat).
- Count one repetition every time your head reaches an end range of motion.
- Perform 21 motions of up *and* down
  - It's okay if you perform 21 complete head nods, but I'm trying to be nice as head nods will continue to be used throughout the following movements.

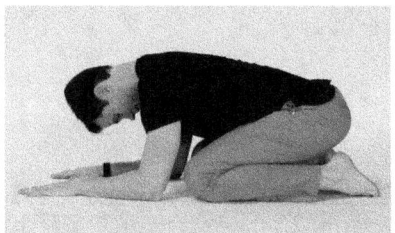
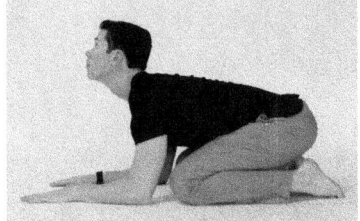

Head Rotations

Why?
- Head Rotations offer similar visual and vestibular system benefits as Head Nods, but they stimulate the visual and vestibular system in a different vector of movement, horizontally versus vertically.
- Head Rotations rotate the vertebrae in the cervical spine, lubricating these joints and bringing nourishment to them.
- Head Rotations also gently lead the spine into lateral flexion, moving the spine as it was intended but through a motion that is often neglected.

A DAILY MOVEMENT ROUTINE

- Moving the spine in all the ways it is designed to move keeps the spine mobile and youthful.

How?
- From the Baby's Breath position, close your lips, place your tongue on the roof of your mouth, and breathe through your nose.
    - Maintain this way of breathing throughout this movement.
- Hold your head up so that your eyes are on the horizon.
- Using your eyes, look left, and rotate your head to the left to where it will comfortably go.
    - Allow your spine to follow your head.
    - Allow your arms to shift or lift as your spine follows your head.
- Then, using your eyes, look right, and rotate your head to the right to where it will comfortably go.
    - Allow your spine to follow your head.
- Count one repetition every time your head reaches an end range of motion.
    - To the right = 1, to the left = 2, to the right = 3, to the left = 4, etc.
- Perform 21 motions of left *and* right

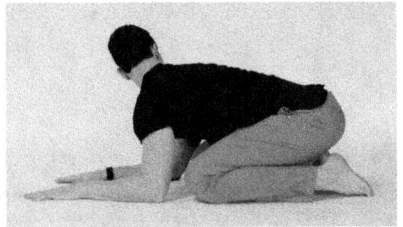

Head Nod-Led Rocking

Why?
- Leading the rocking motion with Head Nods further activates the vestibular system and coordinates the rhythmic motion of the entire body.
- This is a fantastic way to mobilize most of the moving joints in the body.
- This is a gentle way to move the hips and knees through their full range of motion.
- Rocking integrates all the major moving joints into a whole body.
    - It tells your nervous system where everything is and coordinates all parts into one part.
- Rocking teaches the body how to stabilize the joints, turning on stabilizers so prime movers are free to move as they were designed.
- Rocking helps restore the proper curvature of the spine and reflexively resets optimal posture.
- This is a gentle way to take the wrists into extension and restore proper range of motion.
- Rocking calms the nervous system and soothes the emotions.
    - This movement can help the body move out of a state of stress and return to a state of peace.
    - Rocking can help relieve excess tension in the body, thus freeing up energy to be used elsewhere.

How?
- From the Baby's Breath position, close your lips, place your tongue on the roof of your mouth, and breathe through your nose.

- o Maintain this way of breathing throughout this movement.
- Start with your head held down, in flexion.
- Leading with your eyes, look up and raise your head to the horizon. As your head rises to the horizon, raise off your forearms and rock forward over your hands.
  - o The movement is a subtle wave flowing from the eyes to the head, then to the body.
- From the forward position, look down with your eyes and lower your head into neck flexion. As your head lowers down, rock back toward your feet and lower yourself back down to your forearms.
- Count one repetition every time you return to your forearms.
- Perform 21 repetitions of this rocking movement.

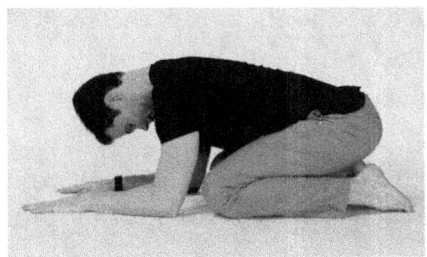 

Elbow Rolls and Leg Rolls

Why?
- Rolling further activates your vestibular system but also greatly stimulates your tactile information system (proprioceptive system).

- Rolling floods the nervous system with an immense amount of information from the entire body.
  - The sensory nerves of the joints, fascia, muscles, and skin are all stimulated with rolling. This provides a "clear" picture of the body for the brain.
- Rolling rotates the vertebrae of the spine, nourishing them and keeping them healthy.
- This movement connects the shoulders to the hips and torso to the limbs.
  - This is the foundation of the gait pattern.
- Rolling is youth in motion.
  - It even feels like joy.

How?
- Lie face down on your belly, with your arms overhead.
- Close your lips, place your tongue on the roof of your mouth, and breathe through your nose.
  - Maintain this way of breathing throughout this movement.
- Rotate your head to the right and look at your right elbow as you reach with it to touch the floor behind you.
- Keep reaching and looking with your right elbow until this motion rolls your body completely over.
  - Try to keep your legs as relaxed and dormant as possible when you are reaching and rolling with your elbow.
  - Let the reach pull your legs over.
- Once you are on your back, position yourself so that both arms are overhead.

- Then pull your right knee up toward your chest as if you are making an exaggerated stepping motion and reach across your body to the left as far as you can with your right leg.
  - It helps to "reach with your big toe."
- Keep reaching until this motion pulls you over, back to your belly.
  - Try to keep your torso and arms as relaxed and dormant as possible when you are reaching and rolling with your leg.
  - Let the reach pull your torso over.
- Now repeat the same sequence using the left elbow and the left leg.
- Count one repetition every time you perform an elbow roll, whether from the left or right side.
- Perform 21 total elbow rolls.

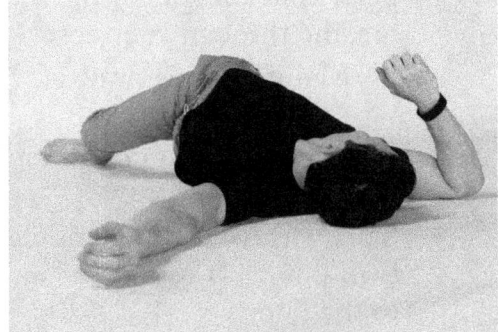

The Rocking Hindu Push-Up

Why?
- This movement mobilizes the entire body and nourishes all the major joints.
- It is a gentle way to take the spine and hips into extension.
- The Rocking Hindu Push-Up continues to activate the vestibular system and coordinates the movement of the entire body in a fluid, wave-like fashion.
  - It's a flowing movement.
  - Movements that flow allow your emotions and thoughts to become "light."

How?
- From the Baby's Breath position, close your lips, place your tongue on the roof of your mouth, and breathe through your nose.
  - Maintain this way of breathing throughout this movement.
- Place your feet in dorsiflexion (get on the balls of your feet).
- Start with your head held down so that your neck is in line with your spine and your face is parallel to the floor.
- Leading with your eyes, you are going to dive down to the floor and rise out of the dive as you raise your head up to the sky.
  - As your head rises to the sky, press your arms to the floor and allow your spine to extend.
  - As your spine extends, your hips will follow, and they will open up into extension.

- The movement is a fluid wave flowing from the eyes to the head, to the spine, to the hips.
- From the up (Cobra) position, look down with your eyes, lower your head, and push your hips back toward your feet and lower yourself back down to your forearms.
- Count one repetition every time you return to your forearms.
- Perform 21 repetitions of the Rocking Hindu Push-Up.

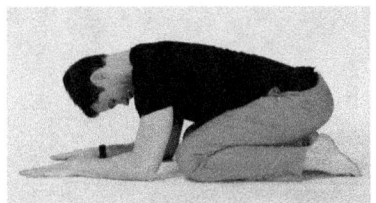

Up and Overs

Why?
- Up and Overs further activates your vestibular system and greatly stimulates your tactile information system (proprioceptive system).
- Like rolling, Up and Overs flood the nervous system with an immense amount of information from the entire body.

- Up and Overs teach the body how to fall backward and protect the head. This is vital for longevity.
- Up and Overs help the body learn where it can and cannot move, filling in movement gaps in the nervous system's movement maps.
  - These eventually help the body move free of limitations.
- These movements fill in strength gaps as well.
- Up and Overs are an excellent way to restore the mobility and strength of the feet.
- Like rolling, Up and Overs are youth in action.

How?
- Start by sitting on the floor. Close your lips, place your tongue on the roof of your mouth, and breathe through your nose.
  - Maintain this way of breathing throughout this movement.
- With an upward motion of the eyes and the head, rock back and fall on your back, letting your hips and knees bend up toward your chest.
  - As you fall back, begin to tuck your chin and raise your head.
    - This will actually happen reflexively (at least it should); it's your safety mechanism.
- Once you rock back and most of the weight is over your thoracic spine, begin to rock forward by extending the hips and legs to pull you back up to the sitting position.
- But <u>don't sit.</u> Let the forward momentum carry you up and over your body to get on your hands and knees.

- - There is no one way to do this, but several. This is where you need to play and explore.
  - You can rock up and over into a rocking position, a lego rocking position, a lunge position, or whatever other way your body will allow you to do.
  - Use your arms as much as you need to.
- Once you are on all fours, you are going to push yourself back over your body and fall back to your back like a rocking chair and repeat.
- Count one repetition every time you return to the floor on your back.
- Perform 21 repetitions of the Up and Over movements.

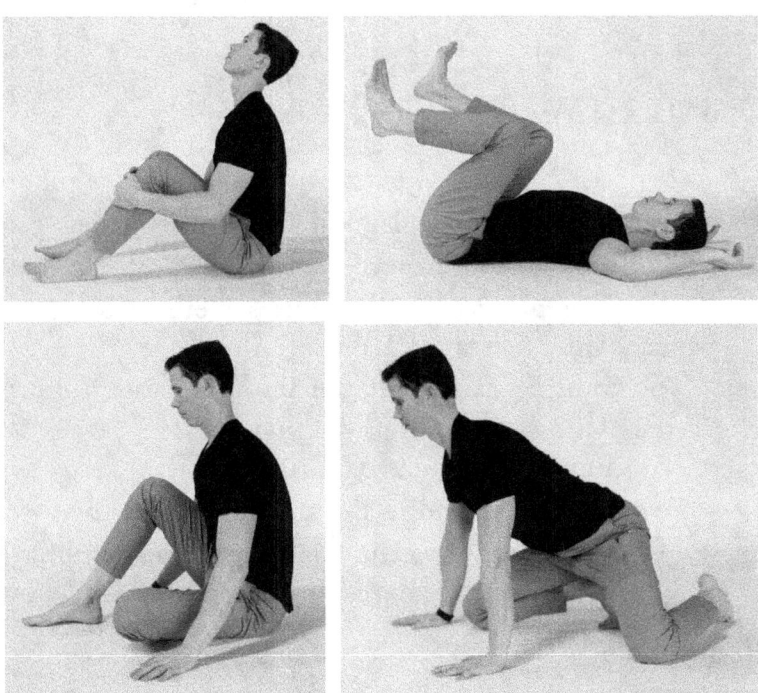

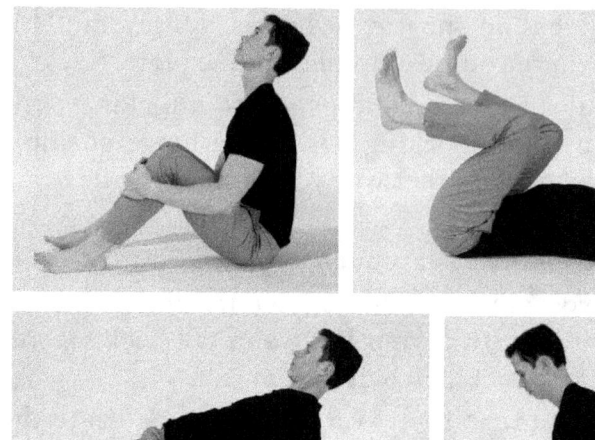

Optional but Worthy: Smiling

Why?
- Smiling releases feel-good neurotransmitters:
  o Dopamine, serotonin, and endorphin
- Smiling places your nervous system at ease, and sends the message, "I am safe."
  o Smiling can boost the immune system, lower stress, and lower blood pressure.
- Smiling helps reduce pain in the body.
- Smiling feels good to the soul and the body.
- Perhaps more powerful than breathing, smiling is a physical action that helps the mind rise "above the line."

How?
- Just smile. From your lips, from your eyes, and from your heart.
    - It may feel forced at first, but if you approach it with the genuine intent to be happy and grateful, you will create genuine smiles full of power.
- Aim for 21 smiles, or simply hold a genuine smile for 21 seconds.
    - Live a life of adventure and mix it up!

The Daily 21s for Vitality

- The Lion's Yawn x 2 yawns (2 different positions/reaches)
- Exaggerated Cross-Crawls x 21 total touches
- Infinity Circles x 21 crosses of the center x both directions (42 total center crosses)
- The Baby's Breath x 21 breaths
- Head Nods x 21 total motions
- Head Rotations x 21 total motions
- Head Nod-Led Rocking x 21 repetitions
- Elbow and Leg Rolls x 21 total elbow rolls
- Rocking Hindu Push-Up x 21 repetitions
- Up and Overs x 21 repetitions
- Optional but Worthy
    - Smile x 21 smiles or 21 seconds

Set aside 10 to 15 minutes to do this every day. These movements are the physical approach to restoring your youth and vigor from the inside out. What I mean is that they do not only restore your body, but they also begin the work of restoring your mind and emotions, helping you to live life from above the line.

The Daily 21s for Strength and Wellbeing

If you have the time and desire, you can also add the following movements to your daily movement routine. Again, these movements may take 12 to 20 minutes, depending on your level of ability, strength, intent, and whimsy. These movements do involve more strength than the Daily 21s for Vitality, but they also return more strength for your efforts.

We are still seeking to achieve 21 repetitions of each of these movements, but the repetitions need not be achieved all at once. We have a lifetime to enjoy our youth. If you need to rest, rest. If you are challenged by some of these movements, and you need to explore them to conquer them, explore away. Take your time and enjoy the process. Achieving 21 repetitions can be done one rep at a time, three reps at a time, or straight through. It is up to you, your intent, and your ability. If you are slowly exploring the movements, you may want to break up the 21 repetitions into smaller sets. You can even break them up throughout the day. What matters is that you get your reps in. How you do it is up to you.

If you have to choose between the Daily 21s for Vitality and the Daily 21s for Strength and Wellbeing, choose Vitality. Strength and wellbeing ultimately come with Vitality. But if you don't have to choose, do them both. Discovering and having extra strength has never hurt anyone.

The Head and Leg Raise

Why?
- The Head and Leg Raise activates the vestibular system and solidifies the relationship between the movements of the head and the reflexive response from the core (center) muscles.

- The Head and Leg Raise adds resistance to the breath, increasing your ability to breathe under tension (stress).
- This movement teaches timing and coordination.
- The Head and Leg Raise, while it generates a great deal of tension, also teaches complete relaxation.
- The Head and Leg Raise reflexively strengthens the entire anterior chain (the entire front side of the body), making a very strong body.

How?
- Lie on your back with your legs straight and with your arms by your sides.
    - If you have back discomfort, a history of low back issues, or a fear of low back issues, start out with your knees bent and your feet flat on the floor.
- Close your lips, place your tongue on the roof of your mouth, and breathe through your nose.
    - Maintain this way of breathing throughout this movement.
    - Do not hold your breath but find a way to breathe with the movement.
    - It may help to find "your rhythm" of breath and match your breathing with this movement.
    - Experiment, but don't hold your breath.
- At the same time, lift your head and legs off the floor and raise them both as high as they want to go.
    - With the head raised, tuck your chin to your neck.
- Feel free to pause at the top and breathe a time or three.

- Then lower your legs and head together.
  - They should both reach the ground together at the same time.
  - This can be a challenge due to the length discrepancy of the legs and the neck, but this is where learning happens.
- Once the head and legs reach the floor, completely relax them and all the muscles that were used to manage them; let go of all tension.
- Count one repetition every time you return your head and legs to the floor, and relax.
- Perform 21 repetitions of the Head and Leg Raise
- Rest as you need to, if you need to.

The Swinging Tabletop

Why?
- Like the Head and Leg Raise, the Swinging Tabletop activates the vestibular system and solidifies the relationship between the movements of the head and the reflexive response from the core (center) muscles.

- The Swinging Tabletop strengthens the entire posterior chain (the entire backside of the body), making a very strong body.
- The Swinging Tabletop takes the shoulders and the hips into extension. This is vital for the health, youth, and longevity of the body.
- This movement also teaches coordination and timing.

How?
- Sit on the floor with your legs stretched out in front of you, with your feet at a standing width apart from each other.
- Place your hands on the floor beside your hips.
  - Your fingers can be pointed straight or externally rotated for shoulder comfort.
- Close your lips, place your tongue on the roof of your mouth, and breathe through your nose.
  - Maintain this way of breathing throughout this movement.
  - Do not hold your breath but find a way to breathe with the movement.
  - It may help to find "your rhythm" of breath and match your breathing with this movement.
  - Experiment, but don't hold your breath.
- Begin to look up and extend your head as you press your hands and heels to the floor in order to raise your butt off the floor.
- As your head extends back, swing your butt down toward your feet as your feet roll from the heels to the sole.
  - In this motion, you are also going to extend the hips and raise your pelvis up toward the sky as high as it will allow you to.

- o This motion may also be restricted to the degree of extension your shoulders will allow.
- You should arrive at a "Tabletop" position.
- Pause for a second or two, or a breath or two.
- Then return to sitting by simultaneously lowering the hips and the head as you swing back down into the starting sitting position.
  - o You can return the head into full neck flexion with your chin to your chest if you desire.
- Count one repetition every time you return to the sitting position on the floor.
- Perform 21 repetitions of the Swinging Tabletop
- Rest as you need to if you need to.

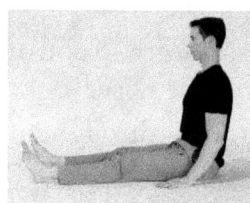

The Waving Rocking Hindu Push-Up

Why?
- Like the Rocking Hindu Push-Up done from the knees, the Waving Hindu Push-Up mobilizes the entire body and nourishes all the major joints.
- It is a gentle way to take the spine and hips into extension.
- The Waving Hindu Push-Up continues to activate the vestibular system and coordinates the movement of the entire body in a fluid, wave-like fashion.

- o It's a flowing movement.
- o Movements that flow allow your emotions and thoughts to become "light."
- Different from the Rocking Hindu Push-Up done from the knees, this version adds "load" to the movement by elevating the knees off the floor.
  - o This results in more tension throughout the body as the movement is performed, resulting in strength adaptation.
- There is also a very distinct wave-like motion when the Waving Rocking Hindu Push-Up is properly performed.
  - o This is a fantastic movement to learn fluidity, coordination, and timing of movement.
  - o This movement teaches the body how to flow, allowing for power to be expressed.

How?
- Get into the Baby's Breath position (forearms and knees on the floor).
- Close your lips, place your tongue on the roof of your mouth, and breathe through your nose.
  - o Maintain this way of breathing throughout this movement.
  - o Do not hold your breath but find a way to breathe with the movement.
  - o It may help to find "your rhythm" of breath and match your breathing with this movement.
  - o Experiment, but don't hold your breath.
- Start with your head held down so that your neck is in line with your spine, and your face is parallel to the floor.

- Place your feet in dorsiflexion (get on the balls of your feet).
- NOTE: This movement differs from the Rocking Hindu Push-Up done above in that the motion starts from the legs instead of from the head—it is a wave from the bottom to the top.
- Leading with a push into the floor from your legs, you are going to lift your knees off the floor.
- As your hips rise, you are going to initiate a "dive" down to the floor with your eyes and head.
  - This is like the Rocking Hindu Push-Up here. You are going to dive down to the floor and rise out of the dive as you raise your head to the sky.
  - On the dive, this is a fluid movement flowing from your legs to your eyes to your head.
- As your head rises to the sky, press your arms to the floor and allow your spine to extend.
  - As your spine extends, your hips will follow, and they will open up into extension.
  - On the rise, this is a fluid movement flowing from your eyes to your head, to your spine, to your hips.
- From the up (Cobra) position, look down with your eyes, lower your head, and push your hips back toward your feet and lower yourself back down to your forearms and shins.
- Count one repetition every time you return to your forearms.
- Perform 21 repetitions of the Waving Rocking Hindu Push-Up.

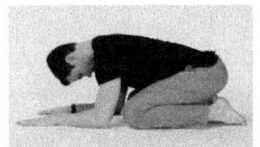  
 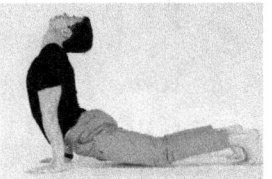

The Elevated Roll Dance

Why?
- The Elevated Roll Dance offers many of the same benefits as rolling, except we are now getting the added benefit of increased tension, which increases the neuromuscular reflexive response.
- Elevated Rolling continues to activate your vestibular system; it connects your torso and rotates your spine.
- The Elevated Roll Dance is a phenomenal way to build strength and motor control.
   - With time and attention, this is where you can learn to master the movements of your body.
- The Elevated Roll Dance makes resilient shoulders by teaching them how to stabilize during internal and external rotation.
- It also takes the shoulders into much-needed extension.
- This is the true movement of youth.
   - It even feels like ability; it feels like "I can" because "I am strong."

How?
- To get started, sit on the ground as if you are "hanging out at the beach."
  - Your right hand will be planted on the floor, and your left knee will be bent with your left foot in full contact with the floor.
  - Your right leg will be straight.
  - Your left arm can "rest" on your left knee.
- Close your lips, place your tongue on the roof of your mouth, and breathe through your nose.
  - Maintain this way of breathing throughout this movement.
  - Do not hold your breath but find a way to breathe with the movement.
  - It may help to find "your rhythm" of breath and match your breathing with this movement.
  - Experiment, but don't hold your breath.
- By pressing your left foot to the floor, raise your butt high enough to begin pulling the right leg underneath the body.
  - You will be contra-laterally loaded, suspending your body in the air with your right arm and your left leg.
  - As the right leg moves underneath your torso, you are going to rotate into a crawling-type position.
- As you pull the right leg underneath the body and your body rotates over, keep the right foot in the air and begin reaching with it over your left leg.
- Reach past your left leg and try to place your right foot on the ground.
  - As you reach your right leg over your left leg, your body is going to want to rotate over because the reaching leg is pulling it over.

A DAILY MOVEMENT ROUTINE   111

- o Keep your right hand on the ground until the reach wants to pull it up.
- Once the right leg touches the ground, allow your body to rotate over and lower your hips to the floor.
  - o You will end up in the "hanging out at the beach" position, now on the other side.
- You can keep your eyes focused on your feet or your hands during this movement if you like. Doing so allows for eye tracking as it provides a target.
  - o This encourages cervical rotation in a "following" manner versus a leading manner. (The head is not driving the roll, the legs are the drivers here. This means the head is following.)
- Count one repetition every time you return to the "hanging out at the beach" position.
- Perform 21 total rolls of the Elevated Roll Dance.

The Hindu Squat

Why?
- This movement has been practiced for thousands of years, and it has been a part of many stories of longevity.
- It is a perfect way to move the hips and knees through a full range of motion with a little bit of load (your body weight).
  - It can be an elixir for keeping the hips, knees, and ankles healthy.
- The Hindu Squat requires less ankle mobility than a resting squat, yet it moves the ankle through a fantastic range of motion that other squats do not.
- The Hindu Squat can be a great squat for developing balance and stability.
- It is also a perfect way to strengthen the diaphragm and breathing pattern without placing bounding forces on the joints.
  - Done outside of the Daily 21s, and for conditioning, this movement develops tremendous cardiovascular health and muscular endurance.
- The Hindu Squat incorporates a rowing motion with the arms along with shoulder extension; two movements greatly needed for overall physical health and longevity.
- The Hindu Squat strengthens the legs while sharpening the vestibular and proprioceptive systems.

How?
- Begin by standing with your feet flat on the floor in a shoulder-width stance.
- Hold your arms straight out in front of your body.

- o They should be parallel to the floor.
  - o Your fingers should be extended.
- Close your lips, place your tongue on the roof of your mouth, and breathe through your nose.
  - o Maintain this way of breathing throughout this movement.
  - o Do not hold your breath but find a way to breathe with the movement.
  - o It may help to find "your rhythm" of breath and match your breathing with this movement.
  - o Experiment, but don't hold your breath.
- Begin by closing your fingers into a fist and row your arms toward your body as if you were rowing a boat.
- As your hands approach your armpits, tuck them under your armpits to reach behind your back toward your "back pockets."
  - o This is similar to trying to put on a jacket by sliding your arms through the sleeves when they are behind you.
- As your arms begin reaching back, begin lowering yourself down into a squat.
  - o The closer your hands get to your butt, the further down you will squat.
- As you squat down, allow your heels to leave the ground and allow your knees to TRAVEL PAST YOUR TOES.
  - o This particular type of squat is done on the balls of the feet.
  - o The knees do travel past the toes in this type of squat. It's okay. Your carriage will not turn into a pumpkin.

- As you reach the bottom of the squat, your arms are going to swing forward as if you are dragging your knuckles on the ground.
- As your knuckles brush the floor, begin to rise out of the squat and continue lifting your arms.
- You will stand and end up in your original starting position with your arms stretched out in front of your body.
- Count one repetition every time you return to the original standing position.
- Perform 21 repetitions of the Hindu Squat.

Tips?
- Breathing
    - Try breathing in as you row the arms back and lower yourself into the squat.
    - Try exhaling as you rise from the squat (as you stand).
- The arms will make a continuous "wheel-like" motion. This motion should be synced up with the squatting motion.
- When squatting, do not allow yourself to "fall" into the squat.
    - We are seeking strength and control.
    - Squat by "pulling" yourself down with strength.
- At the bottom of the squat, when you are on the balls of your feet, try to get "tall on your feet."
    - Lift the heels as high as they will allow.
    - This is a great place to explore to gain movement control and stability.
- Don't rush this movement.
    - This movement has been traditionally rushed and used for conditioning, but that is not our goal here.

- o We are seeking joint health, muscular control, and nourishing movement that promotes longevity and increases energy.
- Move where you can at the time. Don't force anything and be willing to let your body teach you.

The Wave Squat

Why?
- Because the Hindu Squat wasn't complicated enough.
- The Wave Squat teaches sequencing and rhythm; how to move fluidly, piece by piece.
- It moves the hips, knees, and ankles through a full range of motion, under the body's weight.
- The Wave Squat also lengthens muscles as they move, lengthening them under tension.
  - o This creates strong and supple muscles.
- The Wave Squat is another great squat for developing balance, stability, fluidity, and control.
  - o It can be a gateway to unlocking power expression.

How?
- Begin by standing with your feet flat on the floor in a shoulder-width stance.
- If needed, use a dowel rod, a broomstick, or hold onto a doorway to support and steady yourself until your balance and control allow you to perform this squat without assistance.
  - In the beginning, using an aid helps you focus on the movement and not on the stability requirement, which is quite a hefty requirement.
  - It is also okay to always use an aid. Being able to perform the Wave Squat in the middle of a room without assistance is not the goal. Performing the Wave Squat is the goal.
- Close your lips, place your tongue on the roof of your mouth, and breathe through your nose.
  - Maintain this way of breathing throughout this movement.
  - Do not hold your breath but find a way to breathe with the movement.
  - It may help to find "your rhythm" of breath and match your breathing with this movement.
  - Experiment, but don't hold your breath.
- With your feet flat on the floor and your weight mostly over your heels, "reach back" with your hips and begin lowering yourself down into a squat.
- As your body lowers into the squat, begin to transfer your weight forward by swinging your hips over your feet.
  - Your feet will roll from the heels to the balls of your feet.
- As your hips swing forward at the bottom of the squat and your feet roll from the heels to the balls, begin to rise out of the squat by pushing the balls

of your feet to the ground and continuing to swing the hips forward.
  - This will cause your knees to move out over your toes.
  - This will also cause your hips to open up into an "exaggerated" extension as you stand up.
  - To counterbalance this forward reach of the knees and hips, your torso will also lean back.
- Once you rise all the way up, your ankles, knees, hips, and spine will align, and your feet will rest flat on the floor again.
- The Wave Squat is a wheel-like motion on the way down and a wave-like motion on the way up.
- Count one repetition every time you return to standing with your feet flat on the floor.
- Perform 21 repetitions of the Wave Squat.

Tips?
- Breathing
  - Don't hold your breath.
  - Try breathing in as you lower yourself into the squat.
  - Try exhaling as you rise from the squat (as you stand).
- The hips will make a continuous circular, "wheel-like" motion.
- When squatting, do not allow yourself to "fall" into the squat.
  - We are seeking strength and control.
  - Practice this squat while holding onto something like a doorway or dowel rod to learn the motion.
- Practice this squat in slow motion and notice how the joints coordinate in a wave-like fashion

and how the muscles lengthen as the wave flows through the body.
  - We are seeking joint health, muscular control, and nourishing movement that promotes longevity and increases energy.
- Again, be curious and move where you can at the time. Don't force anything and be willing to let your body teach you.

The Track Starter

Why?
- The Track Starter reinforces the gait pattern and prepares the body to express power.
- This movement "turns on" the slings of the posterior chain.
  - It fires the lats and their contra-lateral glutes, and it fires the hamstrings and calves.

- This movement prepares the body's natural shock absorbers (the calves) to receive and produce force in a gentle fashion.
- The Track Starter moves both the hips and shoulders from flexion to much-needed extension.
- This is a gentle way to prepare the body for bounding and springing from one place to another.
  - Youth and longevity have "spring and bounce" characteristics.
- This movement also gently elevates the heart rate.

How?
- Stand tall with your feet shoulder-width apart and your hands by your sides.
- Close your lips, place your tongue on the roof of your mouth, and breathe through your nose.
  - Maintain this way of breathing throughout this movement.
  - Do not hold your breath but find a way to breathe with the movement.
- In one motion, swing your left arm back as you reach your right leg back and lean your torso forward.
  - You can keep your eyes on the horizon or keep your neck in line with the rest of your spine.
  - Your left leg will bend to accommodate the hip flexion, and your right arm should swing forward to match the "forward" but planted left leg.
  - Your left heel will slightly raise to transfer weight to the ball of your left foot.
  - Your right foot will also "plant" and land on the ball of the foot as the right leg extends behind you.
    - This is your springboard to step back up.

120 DISCOVERING YOU

- This movement mimics an explosive standing track start without launching your body forward.
- Count one repetition every time you return to an upright standing position with your feet somewhat close together.
- Perform 21 repetitions with the left arm and right leg AND then perform 21 repetitions on the other side with the right arm and left leg.
- If the Track Starter is foreign to you, watch the video to see and understand this movement.

Great but Optional: Pulls (Hanging, Pull-ups, and Bodyweight Rows)

Hanging, Pull-ups, and Bodyweight Rows get an honorable mention because they require having something to hang from, which not everyone has. However, if you can find something to hang from, it may be worth your investment as hanging does lend itself to robust strength and health.

Why?
- Hanging (pulling) is essential for the strength and overall health of the body.
- Hanging and pulling increase grip strength.
  - Grip strength is correlated with shoulder health, core strength, as well as the health and longevity of the body.
- Hanging puts gentle traction on the joints through tension.
  - This promotes joint health and nourishment by creating space between joints that have been compressed "too much" (hanging allows for balance).
  - Hanging helps to decompress the spine, shoulders, hips, knees, wrists, and ankles.
- Hanging also provides tension on the fascia and muscles, gently expanding them to their full length.
  - This also provides more information to the brain and helps improve the brain's "movement map" of the body.

Note:
- This is labeled *great but optional* because hanging does require a place to hang from.
  - A doorway pull-up bar, a suspension trainer, or some other clever setup.
  - Hanging, Pull-ups, and Rows are mentioned together because they are all a form of hanging, and at least one of these is accessible to everyone's ability.
    - Not everyone can do pull-ups, but everyone can hang in some fashion.

How to Hang for 21s?
- You'll need an overhead bar or rings of some type.
- Grab hold of your overhead apparatus and gradually lower yourself down until your arms are straight, and your grip has the weight of your entire body.
    - If your body weight is too much for your grip strength at the moment, OR you want to really be able to relax and lengthen the spine, keep your feet on the ground but relax your entire body (let the ground absorb some of your weight while you hang).
        - This allows your body to relax and lengthen more than it would if you were hanging with your entire body suspended.
    - If your body is too long to hang without your feet resting on the ground AND you want to hang with your entire bodyweight, bend your knees to hold your feet out behind you while you hang.
        - You can also flex your hips and hang with your legs out in front of you if you want to add some extra tension to your abdomen. I leave that to you.
    - Explore different grips: palms facing you, palms facing away, or palms facing each other.
- Depending on your strength and comfort, you can hang passively by letting your shoulder blades relax and move up toward your ears, OR you can hang actively by engaging your back muscles and pulling your shoulder blades down toward your butt.
    - There is a benefit in both. If you are timid about hanging, actively hang and pull your shoulder blades down toward your butt.

- While you are hanging, close your lips, place your tongue on the roof of your mouth and practice breathing deep into your belly. Try to pull the air down as deep as you can.
- <u>Accumulate</u> 21 deep diaphragmatic breaths while you are hanging.
    - You may find this to be quite a challenge. That's a good thing because it will yield wonderful benefits.
    - If your grip needs a break, take a break. The 21 breaths can be broken up into smaller numbers. Do what you can do. Explore what you can do.
    - If you can hang for 21 consecutive deep diaphragmatic breaths while you hang, you are a beast!

How to do Pull-Ups?
- If you have the strength, and you want to challenge yourself by adding intensity to hanging, you can perform pull-ups or chin-ups.
- The setup is the same as hanging, only you are now going to try to pull your body up through space to raise your chin above the bar or your hands, depending on what you are hanging from.
    - There is also value in pulling yourself up to different heights. You need not always pull your chin over your hands. You can also work on pulling yourself halfway up, or three-quarters of the way up, or even a quarter of the way up.
    - You can also pull yourself up and lower yourself down at different speeds, working "regular" speed, super-slow speed, or even fast speed.
        - Explore your strength

- While performing pull-ups, keep your lips closed, place your tongue on the roof of your mouth, and breathe through your nose.
  - Maintain this way of breathing throughout this movement.
  - Do not hold your breath but find a way to breathe with the movement.
- If you are attempting pull-ups or chin-ups, accumulate 21 total pulls.
  - If you need to break this up in sets of 3, 7, 5, or 10s, do what you need to do. All is good. Accumulate.

Notes about Bodyweight Rows:
- Bodyweight rows may require a suspension trainer or another clever way of orienting your body horizontally to whatever it is you are pulling yourself up to.
- Bodyweight rows tend to be "easier" than vertically hanging or performing pull-ups as they allow you to reduce the total load of your body weight because your body is positioned more horizontally due to the feet being placed on the ground.
- Because they are more of a horizontal pull, depending on the angle of the body in relation to whatever you are pulling yourself to, bodyweight rows allow you to pull in a different vector or plane of motion (horizontally, toward your chest). This helps to strengthen the often neglected muscles of the upper back.
  - The degree of difficulty can be increased or decreased depending on the angle of the body, the flexion of the hips, the flexion of the knees, and the level of the feet.

- Because of this variety, I'll only refer to these in one way: a horizontal pull. If you perform bodyweight rows, explore your strength, and do what you can do, knowing you can change variables to suit your needs and abilities.

How to perform Bodyweight Rows?
- Grab hold of your apparatus and gradually position yourself horizontally under it by allowing your arms to become straight. If this is a true horizontal pull, your arms will be perpendicular to your torso.
- While performing rows, keep your lips closed, place your tongue on the roof of your mouth, and breathe through your nose.
  - Maintain this way of breathing throughout this movement.
  - Do not hold your breath but find a way to breathe with the movement.
- Using the grip of your choice (palms facing you, palms facing away, or palms facing each other), pull your body up by "rowing" your hands to your armpits.
  - Like pull-ups and chin-ups, the depth and range of motion of your pulls can be explored. You have a lifetime to be strong and young, so explore and learn. After all, that is what keeps you strong and young.
- Every time you return from a pull, count one repetition.
- Accumulate 21 total horizontal pulls.
  - If you need to break this up in sets of 3, 7, 5, or 10s, do what you need to do. All is good. Again, accumulate!

Hanging, Pull-ups, or Rows?

You might be wondering, *Which of these should I do?* I've been pretty specific with all the other movements, but here I've given you options. There are a few reasons for this.

1) With all the other movements I've given you, YOU are enough. You don't need to obtain other equipment (minus a dowel rod or doorway) or create a clever way of being able to perform them.
2) Almost everyone can perform all the other movements I've listed. They don't really have a barrier for entry. Pulling your body through space requires a certain amount of strength that all the other movements will eventually reveal to you.
3) I don't know your level of strength or your ability just yet. I know you will one day be strong enough to do all of these pulls effortlessly if you want to, but I don't know where you are right now.
4) Pulls aren't as easy to accumulate as the rest of the movements, although bodyweight rows can be, depending on how you approach them.
5) Explore them all. Yes, that's not a reason. But it's an invitation to explore your strength, explore your breath, improve your grip strength, and learn from your body. Remember, I said they were great but optional. Don't stress over them. Stress robs your youth.

Most Honorable Mention: Walking

Why?
- Remember, walking is the secret of the X. It is the movement of youth and longevity.
- Without question, this is the one movement you were designed to do.

How do you walk for 21s?
- Just walk every single day.
- Keep your head on the horizon, breathe through your nose, swing your arms from your shoulders, and just go for a walk.
- Don't hold anything: phone, briefcase, leash.
- If you can, walk outside under the sky.
- Get after it, as if you've got someplace important to go.
- Five minutes, 10 minutes, 45 minutes—it doesn't matter how long as much as it matters that you do it.
- This is your intended movement for strength, youth, and wellbeing.
- Smile when you walk. It makes it more powerful.

The Daily 21s for Strength and Wellbeing
- The Head and Leg Raise x 21 repetitions
- The Swinging Tabletop x 21 repetitions
- The Waving Hindu Push-Up x 21 repetitions
- The Elevated Roll Dance x 21 total rolls
- The Hindu Squat x 21 repetitions
- The Wave Squat x 21 repetitions
- The Track Starter x 21 repetitions per leg (42 total movements)
- Optional but Worthy:
  - Hanging x 21 breaths, or
  - Pull-ups, Chin-ups, or Rows x 21 total repetitions
- Most Honorable Mention
  - Take intentional walks as much and as often as you can

If you can spare another 12 to 20 minutes, perform these movements along with the Daily 21s for Vitality. They can be done immediately following the 21s for Vitality, or they can be done later in the day as a movement elixir. You may be tempted to replace the 21s for Vitality and only perform the 21s for Strength and Wellbeing. Don't. Done alone, these movements are still wonderful and restorative, but they lack some of the gentleness and, well, "neural goodness" of the 21s for Vitality.

If you can, do both. If you are pressed for time, skip the 21's for Strength and Wellbeing and pick them back up the next day.

If you have next to no time at all (you can only spare five minutes) due to unusual or extenuating circumstances, do this:

21s for Life

- Smile and breathe into your belly for 21 seconds.
- Give one great big Lion's Yawn and finish it with another smile.
- Exaggerated Cross-Crawls x 21 touches
- Infinity Circles x 21 center crosses in both directions (42 center crosses total)
- The Rocking Hindu Push-Up x 21 repetitions
- The Wave Squat x 21 repetitions

This is a powerful bare-bones approach to feeling amazing.

A DAILY BEING ROUTINE

"I hate fear in all its forms. It keeps us from living the way we are created." - Mark Shropshire

"I love you, Tim." - Chip Morton

Along with having a daily movement routine and honoring our physical design, we need to have a daily being routine and honor the soil of our hearts. We need to dig up any seeds or roots of fear and plant the truth in their place. The truth really will set our hearts free and help us rediscover our original selves once again.

I placed those two quotes above because I once read that the only thing that can remove fear is love. Love is a form of truth; they both reside above the line.

Remember, your nervous system wants to feel safe, and your body can tell the difference between the truth and a lie. So let's look at the lie. Ultimately, as far as your nervous system is concerned, the lie is that "it's not safe." This lie is perpetuated with the fear and the judgments you use to attack yourself with: "I'm stupid," "I'm fat," "I'm not good enough," "I can't," "I'm not worthy," "I'm not attractive," "It's my genetics," "It's normal," etc. Those are all lies, and in fact, they are all the same lie just said differently. They are all lies of acceptance. These are the lies we must remove from our hearts. These are the lies that make our nervous system feel unsafe. These are the lies that cause excess tension, shallow breathing, stress, disease, and pain. If we ever want to return to our youth, our original selves, we must rid our hearts of these hell-inducing lies.

Practice Being

The only way to do that is to plant the truth inside of our hearts. Again, ultimately, the lie is that "it's not safe." But the truth of the matter is this:

It's always safe.

That is the truth. If you could let go of all the negative labels you place on yourself, all the lids, if you could love yourself, you would know safety. You would know peace and the amazing freedom of joy. If you used no labels, judgments, or lids on yourself, if you did not allow the words and labels of others to enter your heart, you would feel an amazing energy and vibrancy that is hard to explain. It's the type of freedom you once knew, but it is also the type of freedom you've ached for all your life without knowing what it was.

The only way to truly feel amazing and young and vibrant is to be free of all labels, lids, and lies that you use (and allow) to contain yourself with. The only way to do this is to let them go by letting the truth cast them out of your heart. The truth is that it is always safe. Another way to say this is that you are loved, and you are lovely. Accepting this truth and cultivating it in the garden of your heart is where true youth (Life) is going to be found.

By the way, have you noticed that youth flows from You?

Y-O-U-T-H

Youth is a quality of the original You. If you want to feel amazing in your own skin and live a life of endless energy and vibrancy, you have to rediscover yourself.

The you who once knew no labels is in you. The you that was full of life and endless energy is in you. Think about it. Conforming to labels and the expectations of their definitions takes energy. Living a lie, not being free to be yourself, takes energy. Fear sucks life out of a person, but Love floods life from a person. Love does not cover you with labels, lids, and definitions. Love just envelopes you without expectations. Children have boundless energy because they are unbound, because they are *the* expression of Love. You can return to your youth, your YOU, by removing the lies and their tangling, strangling roots from your heart. The best way to do this is to let Love flow from your heart. After all, "perfect love casts out fear."[7]

This is the secret to the art of you and how you were meant to be. You already have all the energy, strength, and vitality you've ever wanted. But if you're not experiencing it, or if that's not your reality, it's because your reality is based on the lies of fear that you are holding in your heart. Being afraid, defending yourself, attacking others, holding bitterness, keeping score, harboring unforgiveness - it all consumes enormous energy that draws you up and inward. But being courageous and open because you are safe, allowing labels and words to pass you by without defense or

---

[7] 1 John 4:18, The Bible, The New King James Edition

worry, loving others, forgiving others, forgetting memories of wrongs, not KNOWING wrongs—these things are all life because they fuel you with endless energy to expend in the freedom of all the ways you want to expend it.

Does this make sense?

If you want to rediscover yourself and have the youth you were born with, you have to hold love in your heart and nothing else. This is key to the kingdom of heaven, and the only way to enter it is through the ways of a child, through love.

The secret to being this way every day of your life is to know that it is always safe and that you are Love. If you can remember this every day, throughout every circumstance and every moment you are blessed to have, you will find a joy and an energy that people have searched all of history for. You will find your true self. And you will feel amazing.

Remember the line I discussed earlier in the book? You were born above it. That's where you belong. If you have the courage, that's where you can find yourself and rediscover your YOUth.

Your daily practice of being should consist of reinforcing and knowing the truth of your "am-ness," your being. Practice following your "am-ness" with the truths that are found above the line:

I am Love.

I am Light.

I am Courage.

I am Joy.

I am Strength.

I am Power.

I am Safe.

When thoughts of fear, when the lids of lies or the snares of worry approach you, let them go by reaffirming who you truly are. "I am Love." Or, "I am Strength." Or, simply, "I am." Knowing this, testing this (you should know how now), and practicing this is how you allow Life to flow from you and *as* You. This is how you guard your heart above all else (above the line), and this is how you reveal the true program in the DNA of your soul.

If you're not buying what I'm saying right now, that's okay. Just do the daily movement routines anyway. They will make you feel amazing. And, once you begin to feel amazing, your heart may be more open to the rest of what I'm inviting you to explore. Either way, you were made to be youthful (full of youth), full of the original you for your entire lifetime. And that is the message and purpose of this book.

You were young once. But *were* is a verb of being, and your *being* has not changed. Therefore, you are young, and you will always be young, whether you realize it or not. Youth is merely the expression of YOU untethered and unencumbered, free of fear, free of labels, free of lies. Full of courage, willingness, intelligence, strength, joy, energy, and so much more. That's who you are. Youth is merely your true, authentic expression.

Forever You(ng)

I've thrown a lot at you. Consider the things I've said. Test them out. Let your body and the inherent wisdom it contains tell you if there is any truth to these words or not. Do the same with the movements I've shown you. Test those out too. The inherent wisdom that is in you can guide you if you allow it to. If you're tracking with me, or if you expand your thoughts a little, you can test anything, ask anything, and know, really, anything. That alone is an amazing gift beyond words. Can you wrap your head around this?

If you are willing, you can learn to be as open and free as you were when you were a child. To be fair, back then, you didn't know any better but to express your true self. Now, you get to choose to discover (or rediscover) your true self, and you get to decide whether or not you want to let Life flow from you. That's like finding the greatest treasure imaginable in your backyard. That's the thrill of adventure and the life of dreams begging to be engaged. There is so much more to you, so much more in you than you can ever discover during the time you occupy this earth. Fortunately for you, you have all the energy you could ever need to enjoy this discovery if you choose to.

In the end, these bodies weren't made to last forever, but they were made to last a lifetime. They are our bodies, but they are not us. They belong to us. We must care for them and nurture them. They express the life that is us. They express our hearts, our thoughts, and our emotions. They carry out our desires. They give us information. They are designed to flow freely with ease, to feel amazing. But they are merely the living container, the expression of what they carry inside. And what they carry inside is boundless Life, Love, Light, Energy, Power, and Strength—the essence of You(th).

You cannot lose your essence. You can misplace it, or hide it, but you can't lose your true self. Like all heroes, you were born "above the line." Truth is your strength. It yields a youthful life told of in folklore and a freedom sought after for eons. It allows you to feel amazing in your body, mind, and soul. False information (fear) is your kryptonite. Sown in your heart, below the line, fear consumes you, ages you, and ravages you from the inside out.

The truth is that what once was, always is. You can rediscover your true self. The original light, energy, and joy you once had is still there. The youth you were born with is still in you. It is still you. That's the truth. And you can test it.

www.ingramcontent.com/pod-product-compliance
Lightning Source LLC
Chambersburg PA
CBHW071504080526
44587CB00014B/2207